The BOOK of WEIRD

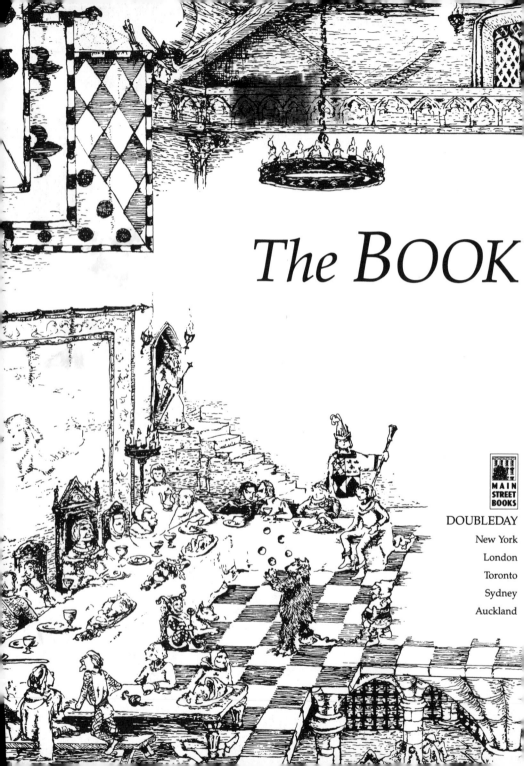

The BOOK

MAIN STREET BOOKS

DOUBLEDAY

New York
London
Toronto
Sydney
Auckland

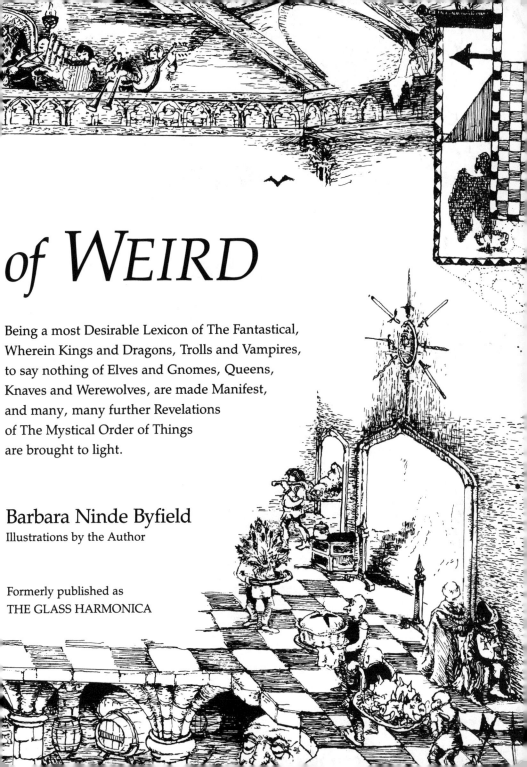

of WEIRD

Being a most Desirable Lexicon of The Fantastical,
Wherein Kings and Dragons, Trolls and Vampires,
to say nothing of Elves and Gnomes, Queens,
Knaves and Werewolves, are made Manifest,
and many, many further Revelations
of The Mystical Order of Things
are brought to light.

Barbara Ninde Byfield
Illustrations by the Author

Formerly published as
THE GLASS HARMONICA

A MAIN STREET BOOK
PUBLISHED BY DOUBLEDAY
a division of Bantam Doubleday Dell Publishing Group, Inc.
1540 Broadway, New York, New York 10036

MAIN STREET BOOKS, DOUBLEDAY, and the portrayal
of a building with a tree are trademarks of Doubleday,
a division of Bantam Doubleday Dell Publishing Group, Inc.

The Book of Weird was previously published in 1973
by Dolphin /Doubleday.

DESIGNED BY HELEN ROSTANGO

Library of Congress Cataloging-in-Publication Data
Byfield, Barbara Ninde.
  [Glass harmonica]
  The book of weird: being a most desirable lexicon
of the fantastical . . . /Barbara Ninde Byfield; illus-
trations by the author.
      p.   cm.
  "A Main Street book."
  "October 1994."
  Originally published: The glass harmonica:
Garden City, N.Y.: Doubleday, 1973.
  1. American wit and humor.   I. Title.
PN6162.B9 1994   94-6573
818'.5407—dc20   CIP

ISBN 0-385-06591-4
Copyright © 1967 by Barbara Ninde Byfield

Contents

For

Mother and Daddy
Timmy and Henry

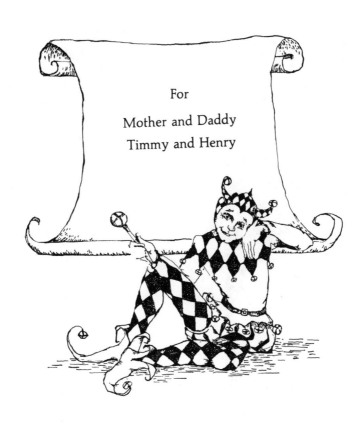

Advisors

SOOTHSAYERS often are blind, at least in one eye, and almost always are ragged. They dart out from the crowd as you pass through, clutch or pluck at your sleeve, and foretell one or two very important things having to do with you alone. These they tell because they know them, and not for money, but it is polite to give them a few coppers.

FORTUNE-TELLERS, Crystal Gazers, Tea-leaf-Card-Palm Readers, Astrologers: It is necessary to go to them, for they work sitting down and need their tools about them. Their advice and predictions are more general than that of a Soothsayer and cover a longer period of time. It is expected that you cross their palms with silver.

ORACLES: The best Oracles cannot be sent for; they do their work in caves or temples which are very difficult to reach and are finally found on a mountaintop or in a Grove. Ask them only one or three very important questions. The answers may be a long time

coming, for the Oracle must put itself in touch with the Gods by eating, bathing, drinking, or sleeping in order to find out the divine intentions. While the Oracle is thus occupied you may be given small tasks or rites to perform.

The answers may be incomprehensible when they are finally given, but later they will be seen to be accurate. It is not necessary to see the Oracle, for it may live in a jar or pot or have only a voice and no body.

Oracles are not paid; they are presented with offerings.

AUGURS: Augurs are not born as such but are appointed officials of a very high level in charge of reporting the opinion of the Gods on matters of state. Their duty is to observe and interpret signs of approval or disapproval as shown by the Gods through Auspices: bird flights, lightning flashes, entrails of sacrificed animals. A conscientious Augur observes these signs at the appropriate time and place: midnight to dawn in front of a tent on the middle of a plain. Augurs are well rewarded by the State and therefore can be bribed.

AUSPICES, OMENS, AEGISES, PORTENTS

AUSPICES are generally favorable, as opposed to Omens, which seldom are, and Portents, which are ambiguous. To be under the Auspices of a King is to be under his benevolent attention. To be under a King's Aegis is more passive, the Aegis being only protective —rather like being allowed to share the royal umbrella in a rainstorm. The ·King's Auspices are much better to be under—more like being given an umbrella of your own so you can continue doing what you had planned.

Alchemists

THERE is a great deal more to Alchemists than simply saying that they are people who live in stone houses and blow glass.

The practice of Alchemy presupposes a laboratory full of precisely manufactured vessels and instruments few of which can be purchased even for ready money, supplies of exotic as well as everyday nature, and privacy, and having a good floor drain. Since Alchemists seldom have cash on hand, their laboratories and adjacent dwellings are commonly located in the basements of narrow stone houses at the end of obscure streets. There rents are low, ceilings high, and visitors infrequent.

Turning base metal not only into gold but into the finest gold, measured by quarters of wheat grains, is only the first step, albeit the Magnum Opus, of Alchemists. When they have achieved this they are entitled to call themselves Adepts, to take new names, and to put their Apprentices in pointed hats.

If their Alchemy surmounts this plateau, which it must if it is truly Alchemy, it is concerned with achieving perfect knowledge of every thing. It is best sought under the baleful glare of stuffed crocodiles, surrounded by pentacles, herbs, crucibles, athanors, salamanders, copper-bound tomes, elemental elixirs, alembics. For in all aspects of earth, fire, water, and air Alchemists seek facts, if not wisdom.

Alchemists are busy men and benefit much from the assistance of their Apprentices. Alchemy is transmittable from master to disciple and is not successfully practiced from books alone.

Alchemists write in a crabbed cypher tomes and tracts but do not publish them. They speak well only of Sages dead 300 years or more and have few friends, for they are secret men, men little involved in the affairs of the outside world. From their solitary habits, from the telltale gleams of light behind shuttered grilles, from the vapors and sounds issuing from the deep regions of their houses at the ends of cul-de-sacs, gossiping neighbors construct tales of atrocities, witchcraft, Black Magic, but these are little true.

Some Alchemists achieve immortality through Elixirs of Life; others when dead are found to have buried their treasures underneath houses which have since been torn down and the exact locations of which have been lost.

Alchemists cherish secret passions for enthralled maidens who spin straw into gold, but if they marry, it is with a thrifty, patient housewife who does not interfere and is content with a silver wedding ring.

12

A MODEST
TOWN HOUSE

THIS small town house has been successfully adapted for use by the practitioners of three or more compatible professions—Alchemy, Apothecary, and Astrology—and perhaps an Advocate or Bookbinder.

The Astrologer will of course reserve the top floor for himself, the Apothecary the store front, and the Alchemist the cellars. For reasons of his own he will prefer to use an entrance from a building next door.

It may befall that none of the tenants are married or otherwise encumbered. In this case the second floor, which would otherwise be occupied by a family, is quite desirable housing for an Advocate or Bookbinder, or the Apprentices of the other tenants. Similarly the top floor, should the Astrologer receive an appointment at Court, is eminently suitable for an Artist.

Alligators

are skinned and used for shoes and handbags
are of the Western Hemisphere and China
are smaller with broader heads and jaws

and Crocodiles

are stuffed and found in the laboratories of
    Alchemists
are African, Asian, and Australian
are longer with narrower head and jaws

Although the location of such a house, within the sound of church bells, is at the end of a narrow and winding street little traveled and difficult to find, the resulting loss of custom for the Apothecary is usually offset by the purchases of the Alchemist, who is always running out of something crucial at the last moment.

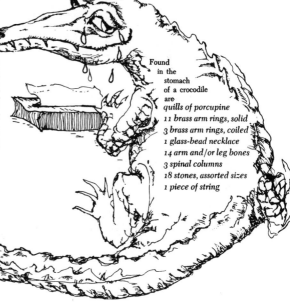

Found in the stomach of a crocodile are
quills of porcupine
11 brass arm rings, solid
3 brass arm rings, coiled
1 glass-bead necklace
14 arm and/or leg bones
3 spinal columns
18 stones, assorted sizes
1 piece of string

Almanacs

Alms, the Dole and Vails

TALES are told that this word once meant "where camels kneel," a campsite; then the climate of that place; then the weather; and it finally came to describe yearbooks foretelling the weather. These publications were expanded to include not only prognostications about weather but information about tides, eclipses, visitations of comets, tax payments due, sittings of court, holidays, the most propitious times to plant crops, and when to expect them to freeze.

Almanacs are printed in many different and very small typefaces quite close together, making them very hard for camels to read.

ALMS are anything given to the poor, especially coins or food, to relieve the sufferings of the unfortunate and/or to make the giver feel better.

Almsboxes are placed in or just outside of churches for parishioners to slip coins into for the poor. These boxes are frequently robbed by desperate men of essentially good heart.

Almsbowls and Almsdishes should never be confused. The Almsdish is a large dented (if pewter) or cracked (if wood) basin passed around prosperous dinner tables for gifts of food and leftovers for the poor waiting in the cold or rain outside the kitchen door. Almsbowls are small brass or tin bowls which, when held out by the beggar and accompanied by "Alms for the love of Allah" or "Alms in the Name of God," depending on whether the beggar is sitting on the steps of a mosque or of a church, are intended to receive coins from the hands of the pious. Any metal bowl of more value than brass is considered unstrategic to use.

When crops fail, mines close, and famine stalks the land, Alms become regularized in the Dole, which is not given but must be collected by the starving, who wait for it in long lines.

Vails, too, involve long lines, but their members are the sleek and glossy servants of large houses in which you have been a guest for more than a night. Having informed each other of the moment of your departure, these servants will be found wishing you Godspeed with open palms. The Vails they expect to have pressed upon them may take the form of money, trinkets, and small articles of reasonable value. In return, it is reasonable to expect them to burn the incriminating blotting paper you inadvertently left on the desk of your room.

Ambassadors

AMBASSADORS, adept in games of skill and chance, are to be found in lofty salons hung with silks and lit by lustres. Able to drink anyone under the table in any liquor, they can also eavesdrop in any language, including their own.

Ambassadors sleep lightly and wear nightcaps, chin straps, moustache nets. They are perennially in the Prime of Life and travel in coaches designed not only for elegance but for hasty departures and speedy journeys. These conveyances are fitted with every known aid to ease and comfort and for the secretion therein of their papers, gems, friends, and collections of rare miniatures, snuffboxes, chess sets, stamps, or seals.

Ambassadors wear decorations; like Heralds they do not carry Arms. They like their private life to be public and their professional pursuits to be private.

Ambrosia and Nectar

AMBROSIA, the food of the Gods, extremely fortunate Mortals, Elves, and Fairies, is said to confer immortality. Ambrosia resembles very closely in taste your favorite food, only is better. There is always enough of it, and it should be served with

NECTAR, the most refreshing beverage and the only possible accompaniment to Ambrosia. It may be drunk by all ages.

Animals

THE Arabian Dromedary Camel is one-humped, fast-paced, and of difficult disposition because his portrait on cigarette packages has gone to his head.

The Asian Bactrian Camel is two-humped and humphs along very slowly as the backbone of caravans.

The Bison is the animal found on Buffalo nickels.

Mammoths, which have curving tusks, and Mastodons share a talent for being drawn on the walls of caves and for becoming stuck in tar pits or preserved in glaciers.

15

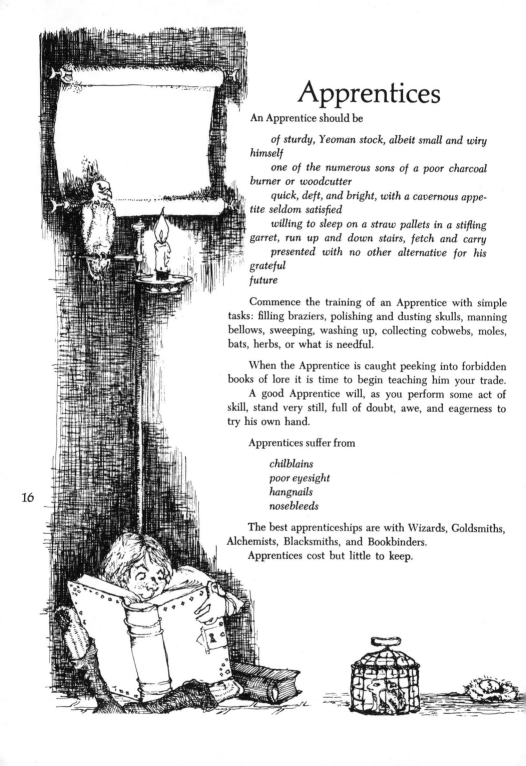

Apprentices

An Apprentice should be

> *of sturdy, Yeoman stock, albeit small and wiry himself*
>
> *one of the numerous sons of a poor charcoal burner or woodcutter*
>
> *quick, deft, and bright, with a cavernous appetite seldom satisfied*
>
> *willing to sleep on a straw pallets in a stifling garret, run up and down stairs, fetch and carry*
>
> *presented with no other alternative for his grateful*
>
> *future*

Commence the training of an Apprentice with simple tasks: filling braziers, polishing and dusting skulls, manning bellows, sweeping, washing up, collecting cobwebs, moles, bats, herbs, or what is needful.

When the Apprentice is caught peeking into forbidden books of lore it is time to begin teaching him your trade.

A good Apprentice will, as you perform some act of skill, stand very still, full of doubt, awe, and eagerness to try his own hand.

Apprentices suffer from

> *chilblains*
> *poor eyesight*
> *hangnails*
> *nosebleeds*

The best apprenticeships are with Wizards, Goldsmiths, Alchemists, Blacksmiths, and Bookbinders.

Apprentices cost but little to keep.

APPRENTICES' TOOLS

ALEMBIC: The vessel or combination of vessels used by Alchemists and Apothecaries for distillation of liquors and waters. It is what the Apprentice must keep the fire going under at all costs.

ATHANOR: The Alchemists furnace, in theory self-feeding and maintaining an even and digesting heat but which in fact requires ceaseless stoking, poking, and shaking.

ASPERGILLUM: Used to evoke or dampen unruly Spirits by the sprinkling of scented or sanctified waters, it can be a simple brush or sponge on the end of a pole or a costly perforated silver sphere.

ARMILLARY SPHERES require daily dusting by Apprentices, for they are the inevitable place for cobs and their webs to gather. It is in the nature of Apprentices not to comprehend the uses of the Armillary Sphere.

BRIMSTONE: Sulphur, particularly the liquid and fuming variety, and the smellier the better.

AQUA REGIA: Indispensable to the Alchemist and to anyone else who wants something fuming and foaming. A mixture of nitric and hydrochloric acids in a one-to-three proportion, it will dissolve gold as well as olives.

Armor

ARMOR, which is worn or carried for the purpose of warding off the effects of the Arms of others, is also worn to gain you entrée into situations where the above is likely to occur. Do not wear Armor if you do not wish to fight. Its presence evokes strife of a heroic quality.

Full Plate Armor should look quite splendid, heavy, and rare. It should be made of many pieces, all of which have buckles and fastenings. It will be made for you by an Armorer and his sons who work in dark, low-ceilinged forges; it will be costly. Sometimes it is a gift from a King or your father; in any event the money to pay for it is always found.

When you grow old, or retire, or die, it can be hung on a staircase, given to a museum, or passed on to your son. If you die in it on the field of battle, it may be stripped off you bit by bit by common soldiers who have none of their own. Those who die of shame or grief

in woods, forests, or solitary towers are found much later in Armor well rusted, turned to bone, and covered with leaves. If you are bricked up alive and left to die, the Armor tends not to rust but to become very dim.

Except on the field of battle, Questing, or jousting, Full-Plate Armor is considered bad taste. Everyday wear calls for an epaule or two, a modest breastplate, and a head-piece such as a helmet. Helms are strictly reserved for Full Armor. A brigandine or mail shirt worn over an innocent doublet, a small plate or mail skullcap lining one's peruke or houppelande are quite sufficient protection when accompanied by a watchful eye and a hand never far from sword or dagger hilt.

In this less ostentatious mode of self-pro-tection one can move quickly and quietly from occasion to event and always be prop-erly dressed whether it be masked ball, at-tendance in a courtroom, levee, church, or backstair. Yet one can, at a moment's notice, comfortably leap upon a waiting horse or into a gondola or longboat, woo a Lady, seize or stow away aboard a galleon, or duel to the death.

The best mail, whether full suit or simple hauberk, should never shine but rather glint subtly with a blue-black light. To this end keep it well oiled, using it as a napkin at mealtimes. Vikings protect the chests of their mail shirts with lavish beards; shorter-bearded Crusaders must perforce wear surcoats. All wearers of mail find it more comfortable if padded gambesons are worn beneath.

Of all Armor, Magic Armor is the most uncommon. When it exists at all, the shield, breastplate, or mail shirt is usually the magic article, and while very useful, it is seldom spectacular since it is almost purely defensive.

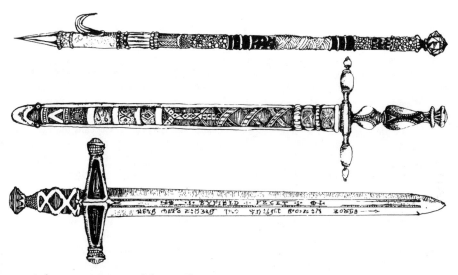

As long as it is worn with honor, Shining Armor takes care of itself without much attention. If you have an attendant Squire accompanying you in your travels he will of course be obliged to spend much time around the fire at night polishing and mending, but if you Quest alone do not be burdened with rags and polish, for the shine will then be self-renewing. The Armor of common soldiers, if they possess any, takes much rubbing, running repairs, and polishing, but it can never properly be called Shining Armor.

Good shields clash and clang in the heat of battle, glitter in the sunlight, and glint in the moonlight. If you are in disguise you may with honor cover the Arms or Badge ordinarily displayed thereon; if you are dishonored or in disgrace you must then cover your escutcheon until by penance and valor you have removed the blot thereon. Use your shield as stretcher when your wounded body must be carried from the field of battle.

Arms

ARMS are the tools of extinction, destruction, or intimidation carried on or about the person.

Swords are the most beloved of these; one can believe in a sword, swear an oath on or by it, and trust it. Swords have names which can change with each owner.

Swords have a way of becoming imbedded in stones or lost in lakes, trees, or treasure chests. Such mishaps do not occur gratuitously; they are the tests which only the rightful heir, the true son, the lost King can pass. If the blade is broken it may be mended only by such men, and once reforged it is better than before.

Blades of swords often have writings on them which is sometimes invisible; sometimes the writing changes as situations change. Attention should always be paid to the instruc-

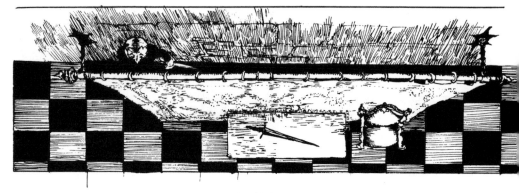

tions or prophecies which adorn the blade even if they are momentarily incomprehensible.

The hilts of swords may contain relics, maps, or jewels. A poisoned sword blade is a resource unthinkable even to Dastards.

A sword may be one, or two-handed. It can be a thruster, chopper, stabber, slasher, runner-through, smiter, cleaver, or lopper; best of all, it can be so mighty that none but you can wield it.

Daggers are shorter than swords, purely one-handed, perhaps small enough to be concealed about the person, and are used for stabbing, nicking, thrusting. They are double-edged and pointed. Daggers are seldom named, seldom magic, and often poisoned.

Knives are single-edged, used by hunters and sailors, and can be carried up the sleeve since they need not have a sharp point.

Cutlasses are carried by sailors, sabres by cavalry, and scimitars by Infidels.

Arras

AN Arras should be hung far enough out from the wall not only to keep contained behind it much of the chill from damp and cold walls but to provide a hiding place for an eavesdropper, murderer, or escapee. It is the site of clammy work, sometimes hazardous, sometimes fruitful.

B

Bannocks

BANNOCKS are sturdy, stick-to-the-ribs un-leavened round loaves baked on a griddle. Made of oat or barley meal, they are a staple food of road menders, wayfarers, cottagers, and the humble.

Baron of Beef

BARON OF BEEF, LAMB, BOAR: The entire section of the animal's back which is normally made into steaks and roasts and includes as well the legs and hindquarters. Servable only on advance notice, it is carried into the Great Hall on an enormous platter by several House Carls.

Barons

BARONS are numerous, active, and frequently troublesome, for their star is the star of war.

Their baronies can be very large and thus yield to the Baron many Vassals, much strength in Arms, wealth in gold, food for armies, and horses to mount his men. Barons

are full of themselves, their dignity, privileges, perquisites, and powers. When seen at Court, they are usually there to ensure the continuance of their mode of life by keeping the King in hand or to seek some cause for grievance in order to betray their Lord to their own advantage.

Thick of limb, dour of mien, great of girth, well housed and horsed, Barons are to be discouraged from assembling too often, for such meetings lead more often than not to envy or treason. Even when pledged in service and loyalty to the King, in battle they may hold back for their own purposes a few troops which must be prized from them.

Barons are given troublesome Marks and Marches to rule in which there are uprisings which must be put down. Barons tend to drink heavily, use bad language, and seldom wipe their feet. Like Dragons they may be spoken of in a whisper by the countryside.

During war appoint them

> Senechals
> Constables
> Marshals

During peace, watch them closely.

21

Basilisks

CONFUSION and uncertainty surround what knowledge there is of Basilisks, not for lack of the beast but because of those who have come upon them few have lived to tell the tale.

The only way to survive meeting a Basilisk is by having a mirror. His look and breath are fatal; it is thought that even the direct sight of him will kill. There are less numerous reports—and they are not reliable—that if you sneak up on a Basilisk and look at him first without his seeing you he will die.

Taking your mirror, back up to the Basilisk. Do not forget that the touch of his body splits rocks asunder; there is sure to be uncertain footing in his vicinity. Show him his own face in the glass. His glance is so malignant it will kill him immediately.

There is never seen more than one Basilisk at a time.

BASILISKS

FACT

have the scaled bodies of serpents
make loud hisses
have feet and claws of fowl
have ponderously long tails
are hatched from cock's eggs matured on
   dunghills

RUMOR

have faces of cocks
have spotted and regal crests
have wings of fowl
cannot fly
are hatched by serpents instead of toads

Bats

BATS consider sunlight vulgar and spend the daylight hours hanging by their heels upside down in dusty church spires, rotting belfries, deserted ruins, damp caves, pyramids, and the better class of dark forests. Asleep, they resemble shriveled leaves, smell vile, and are of no further interest.

Awake, however, they lend great character to crepuscular and nocturnal events such as Sabbats, Halloween, and the commutations of Vampires. Their flight is erratic, flitting, and swooping. It is accompanied by their gritty and high-pitched screams and by the frightened and high-pitched screams of ladies who fear that the Bats will become entangled in their hair.

Bats fuel in flight, devouring usefully massive amounts of mosquitoes and other insects, and when eaten themselves taste much like rattlesnake.

Their fur is home to a varied assortment of Familiars: fleas, lice, bedbugs, worms, and nits. Parts of Bats—bones, wings, fur—are essential ingredients of many charms, potions, and elixirs.

Beaux

BEAUX: Gentlemen of wit and style, or at least of wits and fashion.

Beaux are invited everywhere and go everywhere, caring a great deal about it all but showing enthusiasm only for racing, boxing, gaming, and tailoring. They are fashionable in their choice of moneylender; they set the fashion in wigmakers, barbers, winemerchants, bootmakers, clubs and coffeehouses, weighing machines, grooms, gaming tables, and bookmakers. Above all, they are the fashion with each other.

Bauble, Bagatelle, and Trinket

BAUBLE: A gaudy object, ordinarily glittering and inexpensive, given to someone who wants it very much by one who expects to receive in return something of far greater value. Baubles are frequently given by those who live in Palaces to those who work there.

BAGATELLE: Bagatelles must be given; they cannot be bought for oneself. They are given to impress, the giver feigning a high degree of indifference to their worth and concealing his ire when, as is likely, he is not as well recompensed as he expected.

TRINKET: Trinkets take up a great deal of time in choosing them, putting them on, keeping them clasped or tied, or dusted and polished.

24

Baubles are sure to be made of Pinchbeck and Paste, those sparkling alloys perfectly composed to simulate the offerings of true devotion or to adorn the impecunious yet aspiring.

If they are Fops, they tend to collect small and valuable objects, have more income and go less into debt, attend cockfights, and sit upon the stage at theaters. Their studied languor often hides a tenacious purpose and a wrist of steel. If they are Bucks, Blades, Bloods, Dandies, or Rakehells, their pursuits are audacious and the results much talked of; they often live by gambling, betting heavily on the matches, contests, and races between themselves and their friends. They drive spirited horseflesh and precarious vehicles up and then down the staircases of important buildings, and engage in duels.

Beaux often begin their careers by finding a tailor of talent, or better still of genius, as yet undiscovered by other Beaux. His shop will be found on a side street, the dusty window and rusted bell without giving no hint of the treasures which do indeed lie within beneath the dusty snippets and raveled tape measures: lengths of rich, glossy, and highly desirable damask, nankeen, whipcord, jacquard, velour, broadcloth, mohair, brocade, cambric, linen, twill.

His stooped form covered in ancient and ill-cut fustian, the tailor will recognize in the broad shoulders, slim waist, and shapely calves of the candidate the ideal vehicle to display his art. In a very short time and for very little money he will turn the aspirant out in peerless and enviable creations never before seen but soon to be imitated. Collars will be rolled where flattened revers might be expected; buttons and froggings are placed where no buttons and froggings were before; inventive doublings, facings, and pipings call quiet attention to unthought-of cravats. The weskits gracefully acknowledge that a Beau's reputation can rise and fall on the placement of a fob.

But it is well to look to the future, for one cannot be a Beau forever. The back streets are full of tailors of genius and young men with shoulders, chests, and calves. The life itself is fattening, expensive, and somewhat briefer than other occupations. If Beaux do not perish on the dueling ground, hunting field, or in gaming rooms, they tend to dwindle away, deeply in debt, in an unfashionable watering place shuffling about in a stained dressing gown. Reduced to drinking gin, they wait for a summons from an August Personage they have somehow offended. This summons, if it comes at all, will arrive too late.

25

Bedbugs

Like Vampires, Bedbugs

are most active just before
dawn, and in summer
do not feed on each other
if starving will venture, albeit
perilously, into daylight and will
travel from afar to feed
must pierce the skin of their
prey before they can eat
change color and appearance:
before feeding, the Bedbug
is flat and chestnut col-
ored
after feeding, it is plump,
elongated, and colored
a dark purple
are accompanied ofttimes by
bats
can survive when young without drink for a week and when adult
for up to a year

Placed in a hollow bean and swallowed, they are said to cure fever. Spiders and scorpions dislike them; cockroaches admire them.

Bells

BELLS sound alarms, break lightning, announce floods and fire, mark the presence of pestilence, ban Witches and Ghosts, and call to safety, counsels, and pleasure. They toll at death thrice for a man and twice for a woman, summoning mourners.

Bells mark the hour of *couvre-feu* each night, keeping the restless from gossip, late hours, and sedition. The entire ring marks the passing of each old year and welcomes the new in peal upon peal.

Bells are gregarious and like the company of other Bells. They are subtle, when struck giving out more than one note in undertones and overtones. Bells can, when they please, speak for themselves. They have opinions and they administer justice by executing the otherwise unpunishable guilty caught in their belfries.

Bells have names, they are baptized, their weights and measurements are kept track of in old records. They have a way of becoming lost, but only to be found again at the bottom of lakes, wells, and abandoned shafts when they are needed.

Like owls, Bells comment. Like Elves, they are at their best in motion or when they have disappeared.

Below Stairs

PANTRIES are for bread and for laying trays of silver which are polished there, or of tole.

Stillrooms contain stills for preparing cordials, syrups, scents, liqueurs. In stillrooms one finds preserves, dark fruit cakes ripening, infusions, teas and coffees, pickles, preserves, conserves, syllabubs. In them Ladies' Maids prepare washes, lotions, creams, rinses, dyes.

Stillrooms are reigned over by Housekeepers in black with many keys, and are maintained by Stillroom Maids who are allowed a pint of ale a day.

Larders hold meats ready for the cooking, bacons, sausages, joints, hams, eggs, butter, cheeses, meats corned or salted, jugged hares, aging game.

Sculleries have stone floors awash with tears of hapless Scullery Maids, and stone sinks afloat with dishwater wherein young Scullions scrub pots and pans, plates and platters, but never fast enough to keep up with the Cook in the adjoining kitchen.

Butteries are the domain of Butlers, who hold keys to these cellars wherein are stored wines, ales, liquors, and beers. In them are bottles and butts, casks and firkins, many cobwebs, and a short candle end near the door.

Berserkers

PROPER Berserkers are mighty of stature, hirsute of face and body, generously thewed and sinewed; their interest is not in war but in battle. In time of peace, therefore, they are dour and melancholy, with little occupation save sharpening their weapons and mending their scanty battle harnesses. They are thus inclined to drink.

In battle they will be seen to froth and foam at the mouth, their cry will be that of a wolf or bear, and as they close in on their foe it will be noted that they become lower of brow, hairier of face and limb, longer of arm and shorter of leg, and more powerful withal.

Experienced Berserkers are able to transform themselves entirely at this time, bears and wolves being the most favored animal forms.

Wise Berserkers will provide themselves with wooden shields covered in leather, for it is their custom to chew upon the rims as they wait for battle. Metal shields do great damage to teeth and gums, as may be imagined, and Berserkers' spittle is thought to be more corrosive than most.

If times are not propitious for battle, Berserkers tend to sink into lethargy and untidiness and show interest in little save becoming Werewolves.

Birds

CROWS: Crows are professional messengers, fetchers and carriers of letters, notes, and information. They differ from Forest Birds in their patience: a Crow will wait for days at the crossroads for you in order to point the way or deliver a note. Forest Birds are seldom dispatched by others, Crows almost always are. Their caws, while less ominous than the croaking of Ravens, are not particularly elegant or melodic.

news and facts they bring are generally bad and are delivered in a croak, possibly because they live in far northern latitudes and suffer from colds.

RAVENS: Ravens are reporters of past, present, and future events. They like to predict disasters and do so without invitation. The

Ravens congregate in the company of other Ravens on the crenellations of castles, where, between assignments, their ravenous appetites are satisfied by rations ordered for them by the Lord of the castle. It is considered ill fortune if Ravens in residence suddenly move out, although the only positive good fortune in having them as part of the household seems to be their willingness to eat leftovers.

ROOKS: Smaller than Ravens, they do not have as much sense of their own importance and do little except gossip endlessly on the towers and turrets, waking at ghastly hours those unaccustomed to their cackles.

FOREST BIRDS: These are small Birds like Cuckoos, Nightingales, and Woodpeckers which fly about on their own telling people where things are hidden, what lies in wait, or what road to take. Their song is generally glorious, but to understand what they are saying it is necessary to have eaten or drunk or tasted some special substance beforehand or to have performed some unusually kind act. Forest Birds can be trusted and their instructions followed; they seldom remain long, so listen carefully the first time. Occasionally they are not Birds at all but Enchanted People; if you are meant to unspell them the means will be made known to you.

OWLS: Although Owls are not often news-gatherers they excel in analysis and commentary on current events. Owls predict and foretell on request. They mark the exact time a crime is committed by hooting; they do not intend this as an alarm but as a simple statement of fact.

Owls prefer living in the company of Alchemists, Oracles, Sorceresses, and others who stay up all night. They dislike exercise, travel, and other Owls. In all cases, Owls know better.

Bleeding

WHERE there is an excess of blood or where the veins and heart are enfeebled, Bleeding is indicated. Overly florid complexions may be rendered fashionably pale by Bleeding.

Leeches may be employed, or Cupping, or Opening a Vein.

If Leeching, up to a dozen leeches may be used at a time and the amount of blood withdrawn controlled by remembering that up to two drachms of blood will be drawn by each leech. Place them over bony spots in order that pressure may be easily applied afterward to stop the bleeding. The leech should be permitted to fall off, sated, of his own accord in order to prevent unseemly scarring, but if he refuses to do so, apply a strong salt solution to him. If leeches are reluctant to bite, prick the skin first and allow a droplet of blood to form thereon, thus whetting the appetite of the most reluctant leech.

Leeches may be rented from Apothecaries and applied safely by Barbers.

A Cupping vessel should be of glass strong enough to resist heat; the classic size is four ounces. Wet Cupping is accomplished by scratching the skin, heating the air inside the Cupping vessel with a bit of burning paper or alcohol-soaked cotton, and inverting the vessel quickly over the area. The resulting vacuum will draw out blood, and the operation may be repeated, or several cups applied simultaneously, until the necessary amount has been removed from the body.

The swiftest manner of removing excesses of blood, and the most obviously efficient if more than small quantities must be drawn, is Opening a Vein. This should be done only by a skilled practitioner of medicine or a trustworthy Barber. These men may collect the blood in a brass or copper basin and take it away with them, for leftover blood is useful for bathing lepers and epileptics.

If documents are to be signed and/or written in blood, however, or if blood brotherhood is contemplated, medicinal blood is totally unacceptable. A fresh supply intended solely for such a purpose must be provided from one's own veins.

The mortal wounds of the murdered are said to open and bleed afresh in the presence of their murderers.

Bodyservants

BODYSERVANT: One whose duties and interests are the comforts and concerns of your body: clothes, baths, beds and bedchambers, and the food and drink taken therein either at home or abroad. Trust him with messages, letters, false teeth, Ladies' Maids, portmanteaux, tickets, money, tennis racquets. His

opinion should be considered when choosing cravats.

A Bodyservant will have a club of his own; he will not choose to wear a wig, nor agree to wear livery. Before coming to your service he may have led an interesting and checkered career in other lands; as a result he will have remedies, can find the best laundress, and will know before you do who is cheating at cards.

It is well to mention your Bodyservant in your will; after a lifetime of service he will wait discreetly in a shadowy corner of your bedchamber when you die. Leave him enough so that he can realize his lifelong ambition of setting himself up with an inn, lodging house, or tavern.

Bodyservants may, surprisingly, be fond of the music of the Glass Harmonica.

Bodysnatchers

LEECHES, Physicians, Chirurgeons, and Anatomists employ Bodysnatchers. Sorcerers and Wizards use Ghouls. All may find, if they continue to use the services of such persons, the body of their best-loved friend before them on the dissecting table one foggy morning.

Bullion

BULLION: Uncoined gold or silver usually formed into heavy bars. It is found in the Caribbean and Atlantic in the holds of galleons which are seized, burned, and sunk. The Bullion therefrom is transferred to other galleons which, if the same fate does not befall them, transport it either to or from the New World. Some Bullion is made into gold thread for embroidering robes, banners, canopies, and uniforms; some comes to rest in royal treasuries; and some lies gently on the floor of the ocean.

Boudoirs

BOUDOIRS, from the French *"bouder"* (to sulk), are the private sitting rooms, usually upstairs, of Ladies of Fashion. Here they read and receive letters, gossip, drink dishes of tea, receive close friends, scold or conspire with their maids. Boudoirs are furnished with many fragile chairs and tables, pavé picture frames, patch boxes, inlaid escritoires with secret drawers, and small lap dogs.

Burial Alive

BURIAL ALIVE is an occupational hazard of pyramid designers, architects of royal treasuries and harems, drinkers of amontillado, Monks, Nuns, wives of Crusaders, and black-hearted Nobility of evil ways.

Intentional Burial Alive is almost always a somewhat secret punishment for those who are otherwise unpunishable either because of their high position or the unprovability of their crimes. If they possess a castle they may very well be enclosed in it after all apertures are bricked up. Perhaps one stone will be left out for mercy and food passed in for many years, until, at last, it is observed that it is no longer collected from within. Other Burials for more modest folk may be within a cell, a portion of cellar, or an unused or secret staircase or room. Masonry skills are called for in most cases of intentional Burial Alive.

Inadvertent Burial may be fatal or not; it is usually the result of being someplace where you are not expected to be at an unlikely time. Being in bank and cemetery vaults, abandoned mine shafts, paths of avalanches, and playing hide-and-seek in a clothes chest are all hazardous.

Priest holes and secret rooms are also treacherous, since they are rarely provided with handles on the inside of the door. Skeletons found therein centuries later are seldom chained; forced by the need for secrecy to be there in the first place, those so hidden dare not call for help, beat upon the door, or otherwise make signal until they are, at last, too weak to do so.

Techniques of survival:

For air, lie as still as possible close to the floor, where the air will be freshest.

For food, candles, leather articles (jerkins, baldrics, buskins) may be chewed. Spiders, lizards, rats, and other livestock may be present as well.

Water may be present in dangerous excess or not at all. If the latter, damp walls may be licked for moisture.

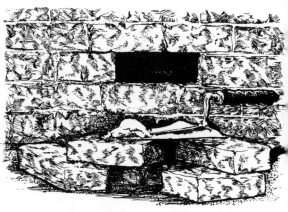

When the point of death approaches, it is well to recall that one's skeleton will in all likelihood be found in later years. Assume, therefore, a significant and pleasing attitude for your bones to be found in. It is well to control your hunger and let the last spider survive you, for its webs will add much pathos to your remains when they are discovered.

Wizards and toads seem to survive Burial Alive for as long as centuries; other people expire much sooner.

33

Buried Treasure

BURIED TREASURE is anything valuable, not only to the owner but to the finder, which must be left behind and is put in a hidden place for safekeeping. A dog's bone is Buried Treasure, but only to another dog, and by the same token pirate's gold is no Treasure at all to one seeking the lost crown and regalia of an ancient line of Kings.

By and large a map is necessary to the finding of the Treasure. The origins of the map will be rather obscure, and it should be purchased in a dingy shop on a waterfront if it is not given to you by someone about to die. The map will properly be explicit in some things and obscure in others; it will only take you so far. The number of paces from one point to another may be listed precisely; if so,

the nature of the points may be omitted and you must then determine them yourself.

Once you have arrived at the general location of the Treasure there will be found inklings and indications not included on the map. A blue flame may flicker above the cache, the setting or rising sun may at a precise moment on one day of the year—the day you happen to be there—strike the keyhole of the door in the mountain which leads to the vault. The church bell which has not been sounded for an era may, upon being rung, set up revealing vibrations in the iron ring of the trapdoor hidden beneath centuries of moss; the shadow of the Great Oak may fall on the location of the proper place to dig.

There is one thing a dead man can do better than a live one and that is guard Buried Treasure. Beware traps: the Mummy's curse, the rock slide, the lantern extinguished by a spectral breath.

Castles
and Palaces

CASTLES, although at first glance cheerless and forbidding propugnatories, are many things to many people.

To some they are prizes to be won, to others goals to be reached. To the weary in the middle of a journey they are a resting place where their tales may be told; to the accused, a court where his case may be heard. To the countryside they are a place of occasional festivity and permanent wonderment, a natural refuge in trouble, and an endless yet logical burden to bear.

The powerful find them objects to be enchanted, stormed, laid siege to, taken, destroyed. The solitary, secretive, or unfriendly regard them as hazards to be evaded, escaped from, or passed by in dark of night.

To most they are the center, seen at a distance. To a few, they are home.

To everyone, Castles are what it is all about.

A basic Castle consists of one tower, the higher the better, with a turret on top if it can be managed, surrounded by a wall. Additions to the basic Castle are almost inevitable as years go by. Moats, barbicans, bartizans, ravelins, more towers are built. Yet it is entirely proper to begin with only a tower and a wall.

A Castle should loom. It need not be built on top of a mountain to do so; a small rise in the land is quite sufficient, especially if the site possesses a rainy climate and dramatic skies against which even the most modest Castle will silhouette effectively.

A Castle should echo. To achieve this effect stone—the heavier the better—is the only possible material. The echo of tramping feet, the clanging of swords and clashing of shields are heard at their full best in a stone Castle; prisoners in the dungeon expect their chains to rattle on stone-floored cells; the treacherous whisperings of usurpers are easily overheard when reverberating off stone walls.

Castles are open, public. Closets, small rooms to be quiet or secret in, are infrequent, but towers provide winding staircases, either exposed or secret, and narrow deep windowsills which give opportunity for daydreaming, eavesdropping, signaling, or lying in wait. Doors in Castles are large, heavy, and bolted or small and unexpected yet locked with large keys. The size of the fastenings is not at all out of proportion to the threat without or the secret within.

Water is found abundantly in wells, kitchens, outbuildings, and moats but sparsely elsewhere, for the natural oils of the skin prevent armor from rusting and baths are not taken. Clothes are kept in long chests and are changed seldom. Castles are lighted with smoldering or roaring fires, torches, cressets, flambeaux, torchères, oil lamps, and candles.

Castles are subject to occupancy by Giants; it is well to provide high-ceilinged cellars since that is where they will spend their time.

The strength of a Castle depends not only on the thickness of the stone walls but on the extent of its storehouses. It should be seen to that the bakehouses are filled with bread, kennels with hounds, mews with hawks, smokehouses with meats, butteries with wine, beer, and ale, dovecots with doves, henneries with hens, granaries with grain, stillrooms with preserves, simples, and specifics, solars with sun, wells with water, pallets with straw, and larders with beeves, hams, and tubs of eels.

Moats should be dug deeply so that enemies cannot wade across even in time of drought. It is undignified for them to do so; they will arrive within the walls in a bad temper, making negotiations more difficult than usual.

Once a Castle has been built it is forever after subject to

capture. The prudent capturer will surround it with an army and sit and wait until the present tenants either starve to death, surrender from hunger, or fall victim to fevers and plagues, which are the lot of the besieged. The Castle is thus gained unharmed. However, this tactic presupposes sufficient troops, food, drink within easy distance, and a benign enough climate so that the men do not freeze, roast, or find themselves weakened with ailments borne on the miasmal night airs from neighboring swamps.

Should these conditions not exist, it is a common tactic to attempt to weaken the defenders by as long a siege as one can manage and then to launch various offensive drives, picking off archers and artillerymen from the turrets, damming the water source of the moat, shooting burnings arrows into the hoardings and receiving in return cannonballs of bread from the starving mockers within the Castle. It is correct to send an impeccably insulting Herald with demands for surrender, as it is to see to it that wagons are busy bringing what at least looks to the besieged like new troops, fat geese, and stronger weapons. The ominous aura of these preparations is much enhanced by cooking succulent and highly aromatic dishes over the campfires upwind of the Castle.

If someone has been placed beforehand within the Castle to open the postern gate, admitting six handpicked men to raise the portcullis and lower the drawbridge for the attackers, so much the better. But while it is possible to win or lose a Castle by internal treachery, a fight is usually involved at some point. When the final assault is launched all strength will be needed and the outcome in the hands of Fate. If a Wizard is in residence the task will be harder, even for a Giant.

As the ultimate battle is engaged, with belfries, trebuchets, and catapults flanking the massive battering ram swinging in its chains, the danger to the attackers may lie elsewhere than in zinging crossbow quarrels and boiling oil and lead. The greed and gluttony of the near-victorious cause them to forget their purpose among the strongrooms, wine butts, and ale casks before the prize is secure and the day won.

More importantly, a secret tunnel from the Castle may have been provided when the Castle was built, a tunnel exiting in a thicket or wood some distance away and guarded by a charcoal burner or woodcutters who keeps a horse ready. The tunnel will have been initially measured for circumference against a small and agile boy whose great-grandson has surely now been sent for help. The help, if it comes, will have lances couched, pennants flying, and very likely aspirations for the Castle in mind—in which case both the besieged and besieger will be out of luck.

If one wishes a Castle, and building or besieging seems inappropriate for whatever reason, it is possible to be given one as a reward. A splendid service must be performed for a very rich Nobleman or a King; these people have many extra Castles which they expect to pass out from time to time to those worthy of them. Worth is measured by bravery, energy, perseverance, and above all success in the Quest, Mission, or Task. At the completion of such deeds of valor one is Knighted or promoted to a Peerage. A Barony more or less guarantees a Castle; Knights are often rewarded with less fortified Manors, Halls, Courts, Châteaux—which are nice to have but serve best as a starting place for another Quest which will eventually bring them a true Castle.

Once in possession of a Castle there will be found certain customs in force. The first is that the Castle does not belong to you at all but curiously remains the property of the giver in fact and law. It is yours in use as long as you swear allegiance to him, promise him military support in time of war and a certain amount of personal attendance in time of peace. This latter task involves visiting his Castle from time to time, sitting in his Great Hall and listening to him plot and plan, and, in the company of your fellow Liege Men, banging your tankard on the table and agreeing loudly with him. He in turn is likely Liege Man and Vassal to greater Lords or a

PRINCE

DUKE

EARL

MARQUIS

VISCOUNT

39

BARON

HERE SHINES
THE MYSTERIOUS
LIGHT

TUNNEL EX

KEEP

LIST

LOOPHOLES

TO THE DUNGEON

MERLON

CRENEL

GYPSIES

RAVELIN

BASTION

RAVELIN

WIZARD'S TOWER

GUARDHOUSE

◄ PARTISAN

◄ BARTIZAN

MACHICOLATIONS

◄ GATEHOUSE

BAILEY

BARBICAN

King and has to them the same responsibilities, although if his rank is high he may be allowed to bang a cup or goblet instead of a tankard.

Once you have sworn fealty and faithfulness, the only way your Castle can be taken back is if you unswear that fealty, or de-fy, your Liege Lord. Otherwise, the Castle is yours, your fief.

With it go lands, domains, demesnes, estates, manors, livings, messuages, rents, revenues, manses—depending on the size of the lands about—all of which are the same thing: the means by which the bills are paid.

If times are not favorable for warfare, Castles tend to change in character. They are plastered and paneled on the inside, the windows are glazed, the furniture slipcovered, and the drawbridge left down at night. Ivy grows up the battlements and it is difficult to distinguish a crenel from a merlon; the turrets crumble. Ghosts settle down in residence and before long tourists are allowed to visit on Thursday afternoons. A view of the exterior is used on a wine label, and *Son et Lumière* sets in.

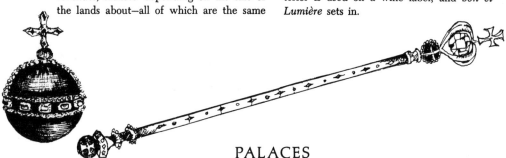

PALACES

FROM time beyond memory Palaces have either been in cities or been large enough themselves to be cities. They are the official residences of Kings, Maharajahs, Emperors, Sultans, Caliphs, Imperial Highnesses, Caesars, Pontiffs, Czars, Doges, Cardinals, Kaisers, Mikados, Bishops, Lamas, and all other anointed and crowned heads. These majesties may be away much of the time, touring their realms, battling Infidels, attending weddings, administering justice in far-off corners of their realms, but their homes are Palaces. It is not uncommon for them to possess one for summer and one for winter. A building identical in size and splendor but owned by one not a ruler is a House, Château, Hall, Palazzo, Manor, or Court; it may differ from a Palace only by the absence of a Throne Room.

Palaces are surrounded by large grounds, walled or fenced in such a manner that it is possible for those without to have intriguing glimpses into the parks, groves, glades, and mazes within, into the gardens where everything is always in bloom and always all at the same time. The gardens may have flowering shrubs of crystal, gold, or precious gems; nightingales will abound. Of note will be a young Princess trailing her fingers in the water of a fountain full of goldfish, or playing with a golden ball. The trees are espaliered, topiary, or otherwise uncommon; the walks tessellated, patterned, and sweeping.

It may be necessary to enter a Palace wrapped in a rug or through a drainpipe, or to leave it hidden in a laundry basket or exposed in a tumbril. But in the ordinary course of events the gates to the Palace are open, and there is much coming and going of Princesses fair to behold and Princes of the Realm, Blood Royal, and Crown. Through the gates move those banished for a time or exiled forever and those who have received their reward and are on their way to the coronet-maker, the moneylender, or the pawnbroker. Out of Palaces come leaders of expeditions and flotillas mighty in intent, and one lone dreamer only the Queen believes in. Spies issue forth, singly or in sable pairs, by dark

of night from the ivy-covered garden gate, indistinguishable from and sometimes in league with spies from the opposite side slipping in. Ministers and their portfolios, Ambassadors Extraordinary and Plenipotentiary, Legates, Nuncios, Embassies come and go, charged with grave concerns, immunity, impunity, and umbrage. Their equipages await them in the drive. Bishops and Archbishops brush shoulders with the man who has come to regild the throne.

Many languages are spoken, swiftly and with ease, and many papers are written: Edicts, Proclamations, Declarations, and Decrees; Missives, and Billets-Doux, Ultimatums, Commands, Writs, Warrants, Letters of Marque and Letters of Patent, *Laissez-Faires*, *Laissez-Passers*, Charters, Safe Conducts, Patents of Nobility, Sentences, and Summons. Some are posted on the gates, and some sent forth by swift messengers on lathering horses. Others, folded small, are pressed into tender palms to be read and reread, and read perhaps again by eyes for which they were not intended. Some are read aloud with fanfare and flourish; some, which compromise

the Monarchy, turn up later and are suppressed, bought back, or stolen. Those nailed to trees in village squares or forests tend to be torn down soon after.

If the Palace fronts on a river there will be a water gate, best used at night by a small boat with muffled oars or by a gay gilt barge crewed with musicians.

As you approach the Palace proper remember that it may have been built of obsidian, alabaster, ebony, and ivory by Djinns, Afrits, or other Spirits. If this is the case it can vanish in the twinkling of an eye, but not until you have had some adventure in it.

As one can expect to find the approach to Castles grim and fortified, one will find a Palace's steps broad, low, numerous, and welcoming. Doors open as if by magic, and one room leads easily to another without confusion. Some chambers will be very large and splendid; they will all have doors. Palaces depend on intrigue, privacy, plots, and secrets; the doors are necessary either to shut out an intruder or to provide a keyhole at which to listen. Secret staircases and rooms abound, as do secret drawers and compartments in furni-

ture and paneling. Palace doors can close behind you without being heard. If this occurs, keep going.

There are balconies of large scale with marble balusters for the reading of Proclamations and Announcements of Births, and for crying, "The King is Dead! Long Live the King!" There are intimate pocket-sized alabaster balconies covered with vines, intended to receive and hear the sighs of the lovelorn.

Palaces endure from reign to reign subject to few changes, other than new Kings replacing the furniture and naming it after themselves. Evil is to be encountered in Palaces; the dangers and hazards are subtle and intricate. Enchantment is possible; Witchcraft is practiced on or by Queens and Ladies in Waiting with supplies brought in by seamstresses from the town. Sorceresses are not fond of Queens and are seldom found in Palaces unless they are Queens themselves. Occasionally the population of a Palace is put to sleep for a given number of years, usually by one outside it, but this seems to be not so unpleasant as time consuming. The occupants wake up none the worse for wear, nor out of fashion.

Acts of mass violence, force, and war are not likely to occur at a Palace, for why else has the King given away Castles if not to have such untidy inconveniences occur in them?

Unpleasantness in Palaces tends to be quiet—poisoning, garroting, knifing, smothering—and is aimed by and at specific individuals.

The exception is when the populace of the town, driven too far by exhorbitant taxation, hunger, and ill-use, storms the gates. Those within the Palace do well at this point to tremble with apprehension. The grievances of the mob are assuageable only by their wearing or carrying away anything of value, smashing or burning that which is too cumbersome to remove, and taking the lives of all within, including the King—especially his head.

CASTLES AND PALACES

CASTLES

Champions
Thickets
Vassals
Guardrooms
Chivalry
Solars
Minstrels' Galleries
Strongrooms
Dungeons
Frogs in Moats
Banners, and an Arras
Jousts, Tourneys, Tilts, Wrestling, Cockfights,
    Dice
Harps
Mastiffs, Hawks, Hounds, Ravens, Rooks

Cooks
Carp, Eel, Herring
Roast Ox, Mutton, Game, Geese, Duck

Cream
Ale, Beer, Mead, Cider, Perry
Black Bread, Honeycakes, Pies

Caudles
Sculleries

PALACES

Guards
Groves
Courtiers
Anterooms
Etiquette
Boudoirs
Ballrooms
Treasuries
Oubliettes
Goldfish in Fountains
Paneling, and tapestries
Tennis, Chess, Bezique, Riddles,
    Masquerades, Fencing
Harpsichords
Greyhounds, Whippets, Falcons, Pekingese,
    Spaniels, Peacocks

Chefs
Sturgeon, Lamprey, Trout
Roast Peacock, Swan, Bittern, Blackbird, Lark
    and Thrush Pie

Créme
Grenache, Canary, Claret, Sack
Syllabubs and Sherbets, Tarts and
    Sweetmeats

Possets
Pantries

PERSONNEL

CASTLES

In the Countryside

Serfs, Peasants, Villeins, Swineherds, Charcoal Burners, Woodcutters, Milk and Dairy Maids, Shepherds, Sorceresses, Armorers, Coopers, Monks, Beekeepers, Blacksmiths, Fishermen, Cowherds, Netmakers, Millers, Haywards, Wagoners, Wet Nurses, Tinkers, Peddlers

Without the Walls

Bull and Bear Baiters, Gypsies, Beggars, Jugglers, Ghosts, Troubadors, Tightrope Dancers, Pilgrims, Bards, Skalds, Dwarves

Within

Seneschals, Sheriffs, Constables, Stewards, Bailiffs, Priests, Monks, Men at Arms, Pages, Squires, Women, Friars, House Carls, Earls, Marshals, Wizards

PALACES

In the City

Tavernkeepers, Turnspits, Linkboys, 'Ostlers, Footpads, Tailors, Merchants, Burghers, Goldsmiths, Jewelers, Fullers, Apprentices, Portrait Painters, Makers of Gloves, Cabinets, Carriages, Mantuas, and Wigs, Cobblers, Urchins, Glassblowers, Vintners, Confectioners, Priests, Pawnbrokers

At the Gates

Fencing and Dancing Masters, Musicians, Pyrotechnicians, Blackmailers, Usurers, Petitioners, Explorers, Alchemists, Suppliants

Within

Mahouts, Chancellors, Major-domos, Viziers, Chamberlains, Chaplains, Footmen, Satraps, Hussars, Courtiers, Ladies in Waiting, Secretaries, Ensigns, Janissaries, Tutors, Guards, Librarians

47

Crowns and Thrones

NO matter how much regalia adorns the person of a King or dazzles the eye of the beholder, sight should not be lost of the fact that there is only one truly operative article when it comes down to establishing indisputable sovereignty. This article may be worn on the head, hand, or about the neck or waist; it may be held, buckled, or wielded, but without it all the other bits and pieces fade into insignificance, valuable though they may be.

This article is generally a Crown, and it is well to remember that the splendid Crown most often seen may not be the true Crown at all. The true Crown may very well be a dingy bit of rusty iron with a handful of uncut gems stuck into roughly cut holes. It may look as if it had been hewn with tinsnips or beaten into linked plaques by someone no more skilled than a languid blacksmith. These Crowns, the true ones, are the most valuable of all, for without them it is impossible to be the real King. True Crowns are seldom seen; they are possessed in reverence and come to rest in state treasuries, where they are given a room of their own which is seldom open to the public.

State Crowns are intended to overawe the masses, lend sparkle and sumptuosity to coronations, provide entrée to assemblages of Crowned Heads, and furnish a setting for gemstones large enough to be vulgar if worn otherwise. These stones have a way of moving about the world, disappearing for many years, and then turning up in the Crowns of various Monarchs, around the necks of their companions, or restored to the eye of the heathen idol from whence they originally came. Crowns themselves are sturdy: they survive being pawned, stolen, hidden, buried, sunk, or lost. Crowns are heavy, thus giving rise to the wisdom that uneasy lies the head that wears one.

People who wear Crowns should be possessed of a profile suitable to appear on coins, medals, postage stamps, seals, and, without the Crown, on pikestaffs, if worse comes to worst.

48

A proper Throne should have arms and a footstool. Armless Thrones lack majesty; armless and backless Thrones lack not only majesty but comfort. They evoke quick justice, rash decisions, and harsh laws.

A Throne should be placed above all other chairs and be difficult to clean under. It is seldom moved, is sat on and not in, and is placed so that there is room slightly behind and/or to one side for Regents or their equivalents.

The ornamentation of a good Throne will leave no place to rest the eye.

A Throne should be placed on a carpeted dais, reached by three or seven steps made of materials both precious and significant.

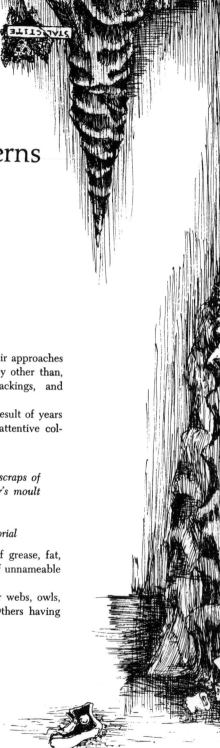

STALACTITE

Caves and Caverns

If you find a Cave, keep it a secret.
Simple Caves are occupied by

>*Ogres*
>*Giants*
>*Pirates*
>*Powder Kegs*
>*Trolls*
>*Treasure Chests*
>*Dead Bodies*
>*Hermits*
>*Anchorites*
>*Oracles*

They are one- or two-room dwellings; their approaches and entrances give no indication of occupancy other than, possibly, roars, groans, howls, moans, smackings, and crunchings.

The furnishings of simple Caves are the result of years of untidiness rather than of purposeful and attentive collecting. In them you will find

>*stones*
>*rough and broken objects of utility: scraps of fur, leather, chain, earthenware, last year's moult of scales or skin, pieces of flint*
>*remains of cooking fires*
>*remnants of meals from time immemorial*

All will be covered in a unique patina of grease, fat, soot, ashes, earth, blood, and the vital juices of unnameable but apparently edible creatures.

Also found will be bats, spiders and their webs, owls, mushrooms, scorpions, and the evidence of Others having been there before.

BEACH CAVES have sandy floors, tide marks, smuggler's marks on the walls, and a gold coin or two carelessly indicating that the Caves are used for something other than fun and games. If you are trapped in a Beach Cave by the tide or an enemy, there will be sure to be a vertical shaft to crawl up and out of. The enemy will not know of this shaft or will not remember it in time to block the exit. It will not be an easy climb for you but you will finally exit in a peaceful spot such as the garden of a monastery or nunnery on the top of a cliff. The good people thereof will take you in and bandage your cuts and bruises.

CAVERNS are seldom the residences of men and Caves often are. On entering a Cave one simply steps inside. Entering a Cavern is not that simple; it is necessary to proceed through a series of simple Caves which lead into each other and are connected by corridors going increasingly down into the bowels of the Earth. The Cavern will be found at the end of a dangerous, dark, and doubt-ridden journey.

As you proceed through the Caves they will be progressively emptier of all save cobwebs and the normal strew of sheltering beasts. It is not always clear which of the connecting corridors to take; it is prudent to make some attempt to mark your path against the return journey.

The Cavern itself when reached will be immense, soaring to heights and depths which befuddle senses accustomed to the close and dark descent. If the Cavern houses Treasure and it is guarded by a skeleton, fear it not.

If forced to escape by underground river you will find the distance to the outside only as long as you can hold your breath underwater or your raft will stay afloat.

The Treasure found in Caverns is most often gold, gems, and magic articles.

There is always another way out.

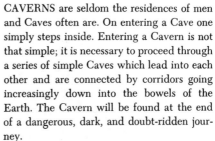
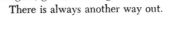

Charms, Amulets, and Talismans

CHARMS: Combinations of words which when spoken, chanted, or sung summon supernatural power to open doors, ward off ills and disasters, effect transformations. Passwords change; charms do not.

AMULETS: Ornaments, gems, scrolls, relics, or remains worn to prevent evil or mischief befalling the wearer. Amulets are ofttimes inscribed with Charms.

TALISMANS: Carvings or writings of a heavenly body or sign on a stone or metal of an astrologically sympathetic substance. Talismans will evoke influences and powers the possessor desires and may be carried in the pocket and not worn. Talismans in good working order are more powerful than Amulets because they grant extra strengths rather than simply warding off illness or misfortune.

Chits

CHIT: A small young girl who may show signs of thinking she knows more than she does. If so, she will be pert, saucy, and forward and will turn into a Shrew when married.

Cottages

COTTAGES are the birthplaces of great men; other times they are the last abodes of the fallen mighty. But most often these simple structures of rude and sturdy construction are the homes of hardworking, patient, and humble folk whose labors are rewarded by a meager plenty at best and whose monotonous existence is relieved by the novelty of your visit.

Come upon in the midst of either desperation or a forest, there will be but one Cottage. The cottager very likely will not be in, for his work of woodcutting, swine-herding, swamp draining, charcoal burning, road mending keeps him out of doors and away most of his waking hours. If there is no answer to your knock, enter (lowering your head, for the lintel is low) and wait; the cottager will have something for you alone without which you will not fare as well when you leave: advice, instructions, a message, an object.

Feel free to share with them the simple meals of cottagers: bread, green cheese, apples, beer, leeks, bannocks, curds, cream, bacon, and parsley, for of this fare there will be enough.

Very small Cottages are sometimes called huts; if untidy, unclean, and inhabited by Crones, Hags, or Slovens they are Hovels. Cottages built of undressed logs and roofed in shingles are Cabins, and in them Witches are not found.

Crones and Hags

CRONE: An old woman, wrinkled, bent, with gnarled hands, few teeth, and a high-pitched cackle. She is generally found in a chimney corner and may be helpful to you in a way you least expect.

HAG: Beware. A Hag, who if she resembles a Crone otherwise, will still have kept a few more teeth, is of an unpleasant and evil intent. She is sometimes fond of the company of one or two other Hags.

53

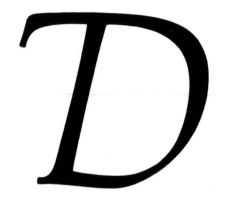

Damsels, Dames, and Dowagers

DAMSEL: A young and gently reared unmarried girl who plays gently upon a dulcimer, attends balls in a domino, and tends to end up in distress.

DAME: The mother of Damsels, the wife or widow of a man of means, the head of schools, orphanages, almshouses, these formidable Ladies of gentle birth must be attended to, heeded, and given proper precedence neither more nor less than their due. They wear rings of keys on their belts, for they are charged with the care of persons and estates perhaps not their own.

DOWAGERS enjoy, after the deaths of their husbands, a certain portion of the estates and titles with which the husbands were endowed. When her eldest son marries, a Dowager must give to his bride the jewels (which she will have reset) the laces (which she will not wear), the castle or house belonging to the

estate, and the titles, and retire herself with her tirewoman to the Dower House. It is at this juncture that she will begin to be called a Dowager—not before her son marries.

Perhaps she will rebel against being thus removed from her former scenes of privilege and perquisites and will take herself to town. Bedizened with bits of lace trailing from a once-fashionable gown, assuming youthful airs and graces ill suited to her years, she will be called behind her back a Beldame.

Dastards and Poltroons

DASTARD: The most loathesome form of coward: A Dastard is willful, harming others intentionally, viciously, and gratuitously in order that he may have his own way. It is he who cheats at cards, besmirches the name of a fair lady, sells worthless securities to widows; it is he who absconds with the funds of orphans, marries for money, writes anony-

mous letters, spatters mud on pedestrians, stabs in the back, and when forced into a duel fires before the mark.

A Dastard tends to be a third or fourth son, if not a distant connection. His vilest act is performed when his back is to the wall, exposure is threatened, and creditors hound him —a combination of events which will inevitably occur.

POLTROON: A Poltroon is lazier and less vicious in intent than a Dastard, more slovenly in thought and less intelligent. A Poltroon can, through negligence and an idle word in jest, supply his acquaintances with embarrassment, misery, and mild disasters.

Dragons

DRAGONS are those beasts which

1. You do everything in your power to avoid. Shun rocky caves, trackless forests, manholes, sewers. Cross streams of pitch only by bridge; better to pay the Troll than to fall into the jaws of the Dragon who is fond of disguising himself as a log footbridge. Ignore the pleas of the Princess imprisoned in the tower, if you can. Come up to the surface of the water from a dive as fast as possible, particularly when swimming in an abandoned quarry.

2. But which when you meet you find surprisingly mortal, albeit terrifying. All you need to do to slay a Dragon is to find one; the Quest which you are on will have provided you with the means of the Dragon's death by the time you meet: the golden apples, the heart of the white stag you slew in the forest, the invincible sword only you can wield. It may be necessary only to put the Dragon to sleep to get what you want, but if the prize is great you will be obliged to slay him. The only surprise you are likely to encounter is how inevitable it is that you win.

3. Nevertheless, they are something it is necessary to get past to win whatever it is you are after. The following information may thus be of value:

Common physical characteristics:

> *corrosive and venomous spittle*
> *which drips from a forked tongue*
> *clanging scales*
> *fire-breathing nostrils*
> *lidless eyes*
> *terrible jaws, with many rows of* teeth
> *scalding blood*
> *a soft spot in belly or head*
> *lashing tail, with stinger on the* end

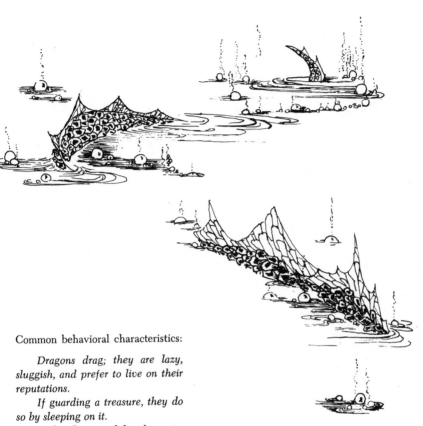

Common behavioral characteristics:

Dragons drag; they are lazy, sluggish, and prefer to live on their reputations.

If guarding a treasure, they do so by sleeping on it.

If they live in a lake, the water will seethe and steam.

Like Nobility, they take place names for their own.

Considering that the business of Dragons is terrifying, ravishing, destroying, and scouring, they are remarkably careless about it and do very little actual work. Only occasionally does a Dragon go rampaging, and then indeed an entire countryside can be laid to waste.

Dragons always appear at the last possible minute.

All of the above is fortunate, for it makes them extremely easy to avoid (have you ever seen a Dragon?) or, if you are out Questing, extremely easy to find and slay (have you ever met anyone who, having come to grips with a Dragon, didn't kill it?).

When entering battle with a Dragon, start from a distance and dash straight and sure at his head, having first drawn your sword. The Dragon will parry with a limb or tail and your blade will clang off his scales; the sound is horrifying and well worth hearing. Several more such attempts, as many as please the bystanders, are necessary. When the Dragon gets you in his coils, begin seeking the soft spot on his belly or head. When it is found, you may kill him at your leisure.

It is well to step back after delivering the death blow, for Dragons die hard, slowly, painfully, and if possible with one last act of vengeance. They need a great deal of room for their death throes and the concomitant lashings and thrashings, bellowings and roarings.

Disposal of the body may take care of itself, for some Dragons when slain dry up into a handful of dust, or melt into a large grease spot, or evaporate. If not, they decompose very quickly and completely. A tooth or two makes a welcome souvenir to take to an Alchemist; a drop or two of Dragon's blood gives courage, invulnerability, and magical understandings.

Dukes

DUKES are the first in order of Nobility and second only to Royalty; they may perhaps be entitled to remain with covered heads in the presence of the King. Their Duchies, even if not independent of the King and his realm, will be enviable in size, vassalage, and wealth and may indeed exceed the possessions of the King. A Duke will be haughty, with fine taste in wine and horses, and should always be taken into account in the King's decisions. During negotiations at the close of wars they are particularly useful in making peace.

Dukes are accustomed to Viceregal appointments or to being beheaded for treason.

Dwarves

IT is unwise to contemplate an extensive journey underground without some knowledge of Dwarves. Unprepared travelers have come to grief in the lands of Dwarves most often when they have not acknowledged or have not understood the following:

Dwarves own all treasure underground, and all treasure that originated underground. Dwarves do not steal; they reclaim what belonged to them in the beginning.

Dwarves own all the underground areas of Earth as well. If you find it difficult to gain entrance to the inside of a mountain, if you find yourself lost, trapped, or imprisoned once you are inside, or if you find it difficult to get out, remember that you are a trespasser the moment you step below the Earth's surface. Your good intentions are your only protection.

Dwarves know more about Men than Men know about Dwarves. When above ground Dwarves put their time to excellent use ferreting out the secret intentions of the world toward underground areas. Therefore when you enter Dwarf country more often than not you will be expected and a policy will have been established for dealing with you. The bitter necessity of learning the ways, intentions, and limits of Men in order to protect their kingdom and treasure initiated the Dwarves' practice of spending part of each year above ground.

Thus oriented, the underground traveler of goodwill need have few fears of Dwarves since he will in all likelihood never see one. Dwarves are not shy, although they are close-mouthed and secretive, but they are extremely busy and have neither time nor inclination to pose for likenesses, run tea shoppes, give directions, or otherwise provide local color for visitors.

Their profession is amassing and increasing their treasure, and creating from it works of fantastic and amazing beauty and utility for the embellishment of their kingdom.

Their chosen materials are all manner of metals, gemstones, crystal, glass, and anything

which can take shape and form under their hand. They prefer those materials which can be found, produced, or raised in their do-

main: leathers of muskrat, badger, mole, ferret are valued by them for clothes, and their babies are dressed in the soft fur of bats. Goods which they do not provide for themselves are obtained by barter with Elves who trade cloth, rope, nets, basketware, foodstuffs, crude amber, and so forth in return for finished metal products such as jewelry, swords, arrowheads, chains, and lanterns. Elfin children receive ingenious toys and games from Dwarves in return for jars of fireflies, the only pets Dwarves care to keep.

The sense of elegance and splendor so abundantly obvious in their work does not extend to their appearance and dress. They are short, seldom growing above four feet tall, stocky, and muscular, with broad heads, wide mouths, leathery skin, and long, coarse beards. Their clothes are uniformly sober of material and color, generally made of leather and plain cloth and adorned only with ingenious but subtle buckles, buttons, and fastenings, which are probably the least obtrusive objects of their entire manufactory. Although they are not averse to wearing the clothes of the country they are visiting, their own dress is acceptable anywhere and indeed is enviable in a damp climate.

Dwarves are proud of their complete mastery of fire and water, both decorative and utilitarian. Their forges and furnaces are world famous. The extensive underground waterways which connect their halls may have been ordained first as a means of transporting ore from lode to forge, but it is not in the nature of Dwarves to leave unperfected any work of their hands, and the dramatic beauty of their dams, locks, canals, and harbors, embellished with waterfalls and fountains, is not the least of their endeavors. When above ground Dwarves make pilgrimages as far afield as Artois, Niagara Falls, Old Faithful, the Suez, Kiel, and Panama canals, and the latitudes of the Northern Lights.

They live under a Monarchy and are capable of forming well-disciplined armies of doughty warriors when necessary, but they are otherwise too occupied to be bothered with holding offices, levying taxes, and practicing politics.

The nature of the Dwarf is such that he cannot be persuaded into any convictions other than his own. Although he is subject to enslavement by magic, riddles, and trickery and can thus be forced to work for others both above and below ground, it is an involuntary and grudging servant that is so obtained. A Dwarf is a willing slave only to his own nature.

In the practice of magic Dwarves have little interest, limiting themselves instead to the manufacture of magical objects in which they delight: rings, hoods, cloaks, belts, locks, hinges, and doors. These wares are highly prized the world over; they are very dependable and very, very difficult to come by.

The common view of Dwarves as simply skilled smiths of precious materials is understandable, if incorrect. When they are above ground, their rather unprepossessing appearance, their menial positions as locksmiths, furnace stokers, helpers in smithies and forges can hardly be expected to give an indication of their prowess below ground.

Dwarves are not immortal. Their lives are centuries long and generally free of physical afflictions other than flat feet. Their women and children are scarce, seldom seen, and silent, but the race is hardy and their numbers in Earth are undiminished.

When above ground Dwarves apply themselves industriously to various occupations. They seek out patterns, ideas, designs, and inventions to take home. To this end they attach themselves to the service of Wizards, Alchemists, Astrologers, and all manner of Engineers. Willing to serve as messengers, couriers, court functionaries, and entertainers,

they thereby gain much knowledge of the plans of Men regarding the kingdoms of the Dwarves. They may stay above ground for long periods of time since they become very involved in the affairs of Earth and participate in many adventures.

Wizards from time to time assign to their care newborn infants who must be brought up in hiding. The Dwarf settles down in a small cottage in the woods with the child and remains there contentedly with it until the Wizard calls for the full-grown lad to assume his rightful heritage.

Dwarves, and their cousins the Gnomes, occasionally establish colonies in caves and hills or attach themselves singly to households and forget gradually about going back below, devoting themselves instead to creating little but mischief. These Dwarves are of the lowest intelligence and are regarded as utter derelicts by the rest of their race.

Dwarves are susceptible to a hideous lust for raw gold which can overcome their normally greater love for things of beauty and skillful craftsmanship. Thus corrupted, a Dwarf will put quantity above quality, mass above magic, and as his hoard of gold grows, his skill and interest in making and creating diminishes. Gloat replaces glee, craftiness supplants craftsmanship, and whole kingdoms of innocent Dwarves have been trapped and enslaved by the insatiable greed of one contaminated Dwarf.

Hoods of Invisibility are the most harmless and most useful of the magic wares Dwarves produce; they wear them themselves at all times (if you see a Dwarf without a Hood remember that the Hood itself can be invisible) and one of the great marks of a Dwarf's esteem is the gift of such an article.

NOTES AND COMMENTS

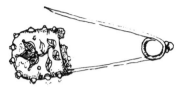

DWARVES most often appear at mealtimes, unexpectedly, particularly when there is something very good to eat in the kitchen. It is wise to share with them.

Dwarves are not frightened by the Ghosts of Men or of Spirits, but they are much troubled by

> *Dragons*
> *Trolls*
> *Men*

Dwarf doors, particularly those set in the rock sides of mountains, are not always visible at first. A magic word or charm may be necessary to make the outlines of the door appear, or they may be apparent only on certain days of the year, and so forth. Occasionally the doors are guarded on the outside by fierce dogs or a captive Troll or two. These can be placated with the hitherto mysterious articles you have been instructed to collect on the way.

Keys are not unknown for opening the doors, but by and large the operative device is the spoken word. It is well to stand back a bit from the doors when opening them because they swing outward. Enter carefully but without delay since they will swing shut before you expect them to, having given you and your party barely enough time to enter. Getting out again is where Men are separated from Heroes. (See CAVES and CAVERNS.)

63

Dwarf doors are still usable even in areas where Dwarves have long ceased to live.

Dwarves possess much foresight, which is to say they know the best thing to be done now for the sake of future events.

Dwarves alone can afford to wear cabochon diamonds.

Earls and Counts

EARLS AND COUNTS are hot-blooded in youth, performing on the field of battle great deeds of valor for their King and surviving grievous wounds. They are possessed of inspiring and memorable war cries, an endless supply of fine horseflesh, and the love of country lasses.

Accustomed to being close to the King's person in battle, as middle and old age draws on they tend to fill positions at Court which are concerned with ceremony, protocol, and administration. When very old they may retire to their castles, where their hands grow blue-veined, their big toes gouty, their memories vivid, and their eyes dim.

Earls are superlative in the vastly complicated Court offices of

> *Chancellors, High and Lord High*
> *Chamberlains*
> *Keepers of Seals, Keys, Counsels,*
> *   Consciences*
> *Stewards*
> *Marshals*

Trust them with all things Privy.

Elves and Fairies

NEVER call them Little Folk.

Elves are tall and Fairies are small: they are quite different from each other. Both are commonly confused with Half Elves and Gnomes, which is the way Elves and Fairies want it.

They are secret people with their own concerns and pursuits having little to do with us. For this reason they may not appear except once every hundred years for revels lasting only a night. If you attend, do not drink their drink, eat their food, or dance with their Maidens. If you do, you will not be seen again.

Elves and Fairies, all of whom are noble and high born, live under a Monarchy, touch their forelocks to none, and salute only their own kind.

Upon occasion they have been enthralled by others of greater power, but the servitude has been of limited duration and of dubious value to their temporary masters. Elves are highly evasive and Fairies are wily. Spirits of almost any sort make better slaves.

They travel more than they stay in one place, and travel in groups, having a great sense of kinship. Although there are reports of Fairy gold, if it does indeed exist it must be as a charge given them to guard and not to spend, for neither Elves nor Fairies carry money.

ELVES

ELVES cannot be sought out. When ready they will appear, but they leave few tracks behind them when they depart. They are seldom involved in the affairs of Men, although they know much about them. They are particularly gifted with great foresight, but it does not concern them as much as the yearly rising of bulbs and falling of leaves.

65

Elves are most likely to be come across in the depths of forests at twilight. Groves and glades, especially of alder, birch, and aspen, please them, for these sites provide quick cover. Although fond of high places, views, and wind, they will not be found above the tundra line, for Elves need growing green things about them.

Pleasing in appearance, they are blond or silver-haired, with pointed ears, clear gray eyes, fine complexions, and fragile bones. They do not become overweight, but move with supreme grace and swiftness and dress in light, soft cloth of their own weaving. They are shod in thin leather or silver shoon with pointed toes; silver is their favorite metal and they wear as jewels opals, pearls, jade, ivory, and amber.

Although they closely resemble Men they are much less dense and are somewhat translucent. For this reason they are a little difficult to see clearly or for long. Elves can become invisible but seldom need to.

They are accomplished archers, ropemakers, weavers. Their kite and harp strings, fishing lines, and nets are beyond price; their swings and Maypole ribbons are a delight. Elves excel as reedmakers for wind instruments. When in need, Elves will ride horses, deer, unicorns. Some Elves are winged but most are not. Elves can outrun most animals.

They are highly literate, prefer song to speech, and their voices, which are light, silvery, and beautiful, are heard at a distance, if ever.

Some live in tree houses, some in open caves under hills. They are fond of soufflés, omelettes, popovers, champagne, and Chateau d'Yquem.

Of them little in truth is known, and of that we cannot be quite certain.

HALF ELVES

HALF ELVES resemble Gnomes much more than they do their larger cousins the Elves. They are in all probability never winged and share with Gnomes a tendency to pot bellies, grossly pointed shoes, and house mischief.

They are smaller than Gnomes, seldom being taller than a mallet. Half Elves are hard on their clothing and seem in constant need of new breeches, jerkins, shoes. Thus supplied, they may work happily for you, although not in your presence. Half Elves in your workroom can change your life substantially for the better.

If Half Elves, who are fond of pranks, prove troublesome and the cause is not hunger or cold, give them useful occupation by sprinkling mustard or flax seed on the floor. They will busy themselves all night counting it and thus the milk will not be spilled nor the horse let loose from the stable.

Their moods veer from truculence to cheer; they are less industrious than Gnomes but as skillful at tailoring, cobbling, horseshoeing, and so forth. Few Half Elves smoke. They enjoy small beer, bread, cheese, apples, pies, and milk.

They are usually found in groups and travel together each year to the North Pole.

See *Gnomes.*

FAIRIES

FAIRIES, the smallest of the lot, are best measured by the size of your thumb. They are winged, volatile, of uncertain temper, and very busy.

Fairies are much more involved with Men than Elves, either setting things to rights or to wrongs. They have an unfortunate tendency to malice and mischief, and even though their original intentions are good they are woefully scatterbrained and forget their mission if the opportunity to tattle, stir up trouble, or inform on someone appears. However, these lapses are usually temporary and it is within their power to repair the harm done.

Normally living in burrows, under hills and mushrooms, in sand caves, doll houses of the better sort, or woods, they can travel swiftly and indeed circle the Earth in the batting of an eye if need be. They are never fat, and if they allow themselves to be regarded for long they will be seen to be quite handsome, dressed gloriously if scantily, and slightly vain. They eat little; nectar and dew, *fraises de bois,* milk, and ambrosia will satisfy them entirely. They are fond of freshly baked loaves.

Fairies stand in awe of Elves alone.

FAIRY GODMOTHERS

FAIRY GODMOTHERS can come from the ranks of either Elves or Fairies. If Fairy, there will most likely be a dozen. If Elf, one.

It is prudent to have Fairy Godmothers in the number of twelve present at Christenings. They will bestow on the babe gifts within their giving: golden tresses, sweet disposition, industriousness, bright eyes. One Fairy will be prudent and wait until the requisite Witch or Bad Fairy has laid the obligatory curse on the infant, and then she will be able, by means of her gift, to ameliorate somewhat the hazards of the future for the child.

In the later life of the godchild an Elfin Fairy Godmother is more willing, understanding, and powerful. She it is who will do what Fairies cannot or will not cope with: pumpkins, ball gowns, pointing out the road of yellow brick, getting you to and from the ball on time.

Elfin Godmothers carry star-tipped wands.

As with all gifts from Elves and Fairies, those of Fairy Godmothers tend to be laid away and forgotten until needed.

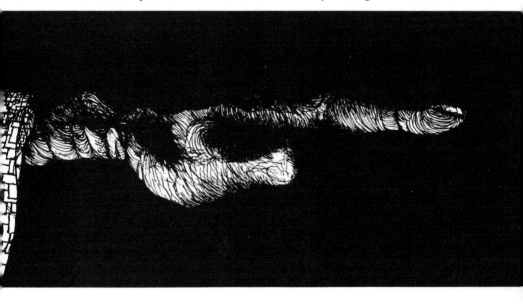

Exile and Banishment

MISUNDERSTANDING between Kings and subjects may arise, born perhaps of treachery, perhaps of conflicting ambitions, perhaps of changing times. If there is not time to Exile oneself voluntarily, Banishment from the Realm, Court, or Presence may be pronounced. It may be for life or for a number of years; one may be free to wander other lands or assigned to a particular place under guard. Ambassadors are expelled, lesser foreigners deported, young men of aspiration chained to the benches of galleys.

Heralds may cut the tails from a Knight Banneret's banner, or epaulets and buttons may be ripped off as the result of a swift court-martial on the battlefield at which the Judge uses a drumhead as a table and disgrace as a punishment. Ostracism is the result of cheating at cards, and although every other bill may remain unpaid, one is cut, shunned, disowned, spoken of in a whisper, and disinherited for not paying gambling debts.

Beyond the Pale, where they languish in Exile, Banishment, or Ostracism, Poets write their best verse, Playwrights turn to other prose forms, Rakehells undergo conversion, and mighty Clerics are at last vouchsafed visions. Those who have been close to the Crown had best return home at the head of an army, under the reign of a new King, or in disguise. They must not be surprised to find shuttered windows, sullen townspeople, thin ale and watered wine, unrest, high taxes. Spindle-legged children, their bellies swollen with hunger, will be seen standing on one foot in run-down doorways, watching fat sheep being driven up the hill to the Castle.

Maids in Waiting who have incurred the displeasure of the Queen find themselves married off to middle-aged gentlemen with estates in the depths of a distant countryside. Ladies in Waiting are more difficult to dispose of and may have to be given the rearing of a Royal Infant or a distant post may be assigned their husbands.

Exorcism

DEMONS who reveal, through lack of either skill or wisdom, their presence in the body of a mortal may expect to be troubled and plagued by Exorcism. The family of the Possessed will first notice the person so occupied suffering grave apprehensions, speaking

in strange voices and tongues, becoming untidy about his person and careless in matters of dress and cleanliness. The presence of a Demon or Demons will be suspected when the Possessed begins to spew forth unlikely articles: stones and toads, serpents, nails. Most families call in the Exorcist when rolling fits commence.

The Exorcist, a wily fellow who will determine for himself and not on hearsay the actual presence of a Demon, will first attempt to make the Demon tell his name. Then, following the technique of a masterful innkeeper, he will question the Demon about the length of occupancy intended, time of arrival, reasons for coming, and the number of Demons accommodated. The Exorcist will have provided for himself robes, a book, cymbals, gongs, bells, gems, herbs, spices, crosses, wines, tapers, and whatever else he finds the coffers of the awed witnesses contain or can afford. Some such tools will be beaten, some sounded or struck, some sprinkled or strewn, some burnt, some displayed. Incense for the fumigation of Incubi and Succubi is very

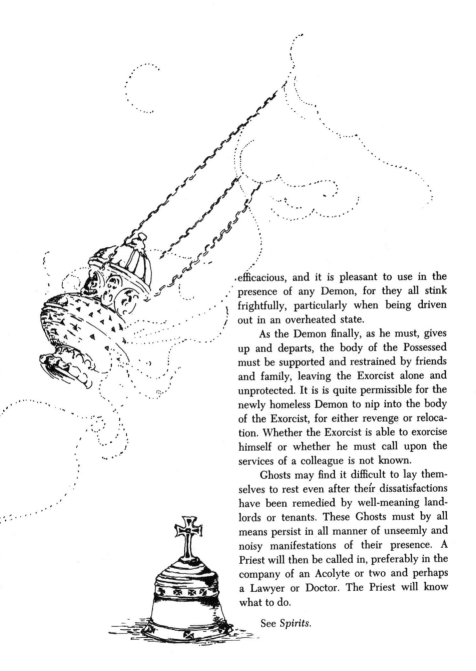

efficacious, and it is pleasant to use in the presence of any Demon, for they all stink frightfully, particularly when being driven out in an overheated state.

As the Demon finally, as he must, gives up and departs, the body of the Possessed must be supported and restrained by friends and family, leaving the Exorcist alone and unprotected. It is is quite permissible for the newly homeless Demon to nip into the body of the Exorcist, for either revenge or relocation. Whether the Exorcist is able to exorcise himself or whether he must call upon the services of a colleague is not known.

Ghosts may find it difficult to lay themselves to rest even after their dissatisfactions have been remedied by well-meaning landlords or tenants. These Ghosts must by all means persist in all manner of unseemly and noisy manifestations of their presence. A Priest will then be called in, preferably in the company of an Acolyte or two and perhaps a Lawyer or Doctor. The Priest will know what to do.

See *Spirits*.

71

Father Confessors

FATHER CONFESSORS are the spiritual luxury of young Ladies of gentle birth. They function as the repositories of hopes, comforters in the absence of the beloved, and receivers of confidences. They are indulgent and absolutely loyal but are easily flustered and tend to lose crucial documents. Only villains of the deepest dye will resort to extorting at sword's point secrets entrusted to a Father Confessor. The office is often held by a Friar whose health has broken down; he is knowledgeable of flowers, herbs, and the secrets so blushingly confided in him which he has already heard from the old nurse the day before.

Father Confessors never forget a birthmark.

Flags

THERE exist three basic flags.

Banners: Square or rectangular in shape, Banners on the field of battle not only are the personal ensign of all those over the rank of Knight Bachelor possessed of a following, but reveal the center of leadership for the force that follows them. Banners are accompanied by drums and are flown with tasseled cords from a pole. From them Archers may correct their aim on windy days, the hard-pressed may take heart and fresh courage; the valiant catch them up to be raised high again after the Bearer falls.

Banners of cities are delivered to new Rulers at the gates; it is Banners which are struck on surrender, or trampled into the dust by the enemy, or captured. Banners may be unfurled where they are least expected; they are cheered, venerated, and wept over by the hitherto dry-eyed.

Charge your Banner with the Arms borne on your shield. In life Banners are borne before you and in death serve as your coffin's pall.

Pennants: Pennants are singular, identifying an individual Knight Bachelor. They invite one's enemy to single combat, whereas Banners evoke the clash of armies; they indicate to one's Squire where to find one. Swallow-tailed or streamered, they are borne on one's lance and are charged with one's Arms. Following a deed of great valor they are made less to become more: the tails are cut off by one's Sovereign, the Pennant becomes a Banner, the Hero a Knight Banneret.

Esquires may bear Pennoncels at ceremonies, Masters of Horse fly Guidons, and the mighty add Gonfalons in a battle to their Banners.

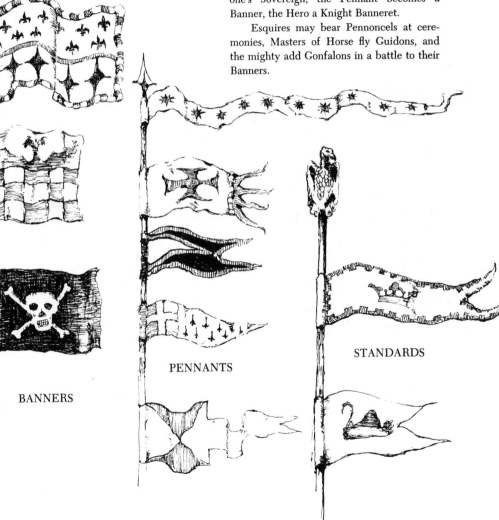

BANNERS

PENNANTS

STANDARDS

Standards: Standards, so large and long as to be unwieldly and therefore not properly carried into battle, float in serenity from a staff above the location of the King's person: in camp, in castle, and if on journey next to his horse. Standards, whether of Sovereigns or of lesser though eminent folk, may be charged arbitrarily with badges, mottoes, and other devices in profusion.

Standards and Banners when captured may be hidden for centuries, and much must be done to restore them to their legions.

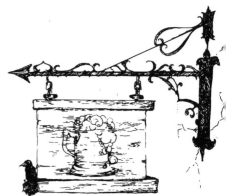

Friars

FRIARS are free-lance ecclesiastics. Clad in a single garment of coarse and travel-stained brown, with staff and sandaled feet, they may join you on the road for some part of your journey. They are good companions with a store of worldly wisdom and will reminisce about their experiences in plague-struck or beleaguered cities where their services were much in demand to minister to the dying or dead. For a secret marriage or baptism, a Friar is the correct officiant. For this reason he is sometimes sought out years later (when, perhaps, he has become a Father Confessor) to identify a rightful King or a long-lost heir. This is not easy, since the Friar may well have become a hermit or been unfrocked. Friars keep questionable company; inquire for them at the nearest ale house.

Tonsures on Friars may be slightly grown out into a stubble due to the difficulties of shaving in cold water without either a looking glass or a fellow Friar to serve as Barber.

Frogs and Toads

FROGS

live under a Monarchy

leap and sing

have dry skin and need damp shade

are sometimes enchanted Princes, Heroes, or other good folk

are cheerful, noisy, and have webbed feet

TOADS

hatch Basilisks

crawl, hop, and croak

enjoy desert regions by nature of their moist skin. They have warts, but do not cause them

are sometimes Familiars to Witches and Warlocks, or enchanted and enslaved unfortunates

have short legs, are sedate, and rest frequently

75

Garrets

GARRETS, reached by a succession of staircases diminishing in width, illumination, and carpeting as they ascend in height, are attics subdivided into living quarters. They are assigned to the lonely, the poor, to old men who hate people and say "Bah!", to old women who have been cast back into the family long ago by betrayal of once-held tender sentiments they can scarcely recall. They belong to young Poets with clammy hands and Adam's apples who do not know how miserable their plight is nor how fine their poetry, and to young seamstresses who are resisting the advances of the landlord.

One must crouch to look out the window of a Garret and see chimney pots, rooftops, and swirling fog which parts from time to time to reveal the brick wall of a house very close by.

There is no running water save through the leak in the ceiling. The forces of physics suspend themselves in Garrets: heat does not rise through the chimneys of the great fireplaces below, and Garrets are bitterly cold. Garrets are furnished in peeling wallpaper, an iron bed, and a broken chair.

Although Garrets seem empty of all save the stark moment, each has according to its occupant some small token of times gone by or to come: an album, sword, telescope, manuscript, or a suitcase packed and waiting for only the visa. And from time to time footsteps are heard upon the stair.

Ghouls

GHOULS, whose food is the flesh of the dead and whose homes are the graveyards and burial places of the world, are at times mistaken for Vampires. However, they are easily distinguishable: Ghouls, if clothed at all, wear clotted and stained rags; Vampires are much more elegantly attired. Ghouls are not liquivores, as are Vampires, and far prefer human carrion to any other diet. It is only occasionally that they take the meat of a living child or the egg of a vulture.

Ghouls can work during daylight if necessary; they are often blind since their senses of hearing and smell are highly developed and they can find what they need without sight. They are desiccated, with cracked lips, chapped knees, and fingers caked with dried meats. Clever, swift, and wily, they are seldom caught at their practices and their presence is affirmed only by the discovery of untidily opened graves.

Ghouls do not disturb Vampires, who in turn have no interest in Ghouls.

There is no known cure.

Giants,

Trolls, and

Ogres

Men and women of vast width, height, strength, and appetite fall under the general classification of Giants. They are divisible into three species: Giants, Trolls, and Ogres.

None are measurable by our yardsticks, having better ones of their own; all are much larger than Men, and there is no limit to the height they may attain. Giants are largest, Trolls second, and Ogres the smallest. All are heavy-boned and muscled; thick-skinned, with hairy bodies, long arms, and large hands and feet with varying numbers of digits.

As a race they are uncommonly anti-social, with no organizations, governments, or voluntary allegiances, and they ordinarily

| Giant | Troll | Ogre | Knight |

lead separate lives as free lances, alone or in pairs. Few Giants marry; those that do have prodigious numbers of offspring, but a large number of the children perish young due to neglect, bad diet, or the maraudings of other Giants, so the race is in no way increasing in number.

They are impatient and wasteful, making little or ill use of the results of their raids and depredations. They dig seemingly senseless pits, uproot trees, trample underfoot whole hamlets to no apparent profit.

> *A Troll will eat an Ogre*
> *An Ogre will eat a Troll*
> *A Giant will eat an Ogre*
> *A Troll will eat a Giant*
> *A Giant will eat a Troll*
> *An Ogre will not eat a Giant*

All will eat Humans, gladly.

GIANTS

GIANTS are the largest of the three species; they seldom grow less than twelve feet tall and can reach any height. Giants are virtually always evil and dangerous, but alone among the three are not necessarily so. A benign Giant or Giantess is occasionally encountered, but it is well to give them ample opportunity to exhibit friendliness before coming within their grasp.

Giants prefer to inhabit castles captured from Men rather than build their own; if no castles are available or suitable they will live in caves, on mountainsides, or out of doors. If they have a castle they make few improvements on it other than enlarging the dungeons for themselves and their prisoners; it is otherwise left to go to rack and ruin.

Giants are fond of ale, resinated wine, and spirits; they prefer grease to butter. Their bread is baked in a hard round loaf made of ground bones that resembles a stone.

Giants are notoriously slovenly, untidy, and unmindful of the most appalling filth and squalor.

Dwarf

Gnome

Half-Elf

Elf

Fairy

GIANT

TROLLS

TROLLS are slightly smaller than Giants and have a wicked intelligence which they bend to deeds of foul cunning. They are extremely strong, agile, and greedy, and must never be trusted. In appearance they are unattractive, indeed, repellent and foreboding: hard flesh, coarse skin, greasy and dandruff-laden hair, vestigial scaling on knees and elbows, thick and scanty fingers and toes, shifty eyes warn off even the most intrepid traveler.

Trolls dislike direct sunlight and for this reason are found living in holes, caves, under rocks and bridges, and on the shady side of mountain passes. There they lie in wait for passers-by and extort from them either by threats or violence their valuables and sometimes their lives.

Trolls eat people, and in time of famine, stones. They are fond of, or at least collect, chains. They are obliged to steal these and other pieces of heavy, rusted metal, for they

are loath to work with their hands. The gold
and rough treasure they amass is well guarded
by them and they do not spend it.

Trolls are subject to sunburn, bad teeth,
and warts. Assume the worst of Trolls; they
are always barefoot, do not like to sit down,
and their blood is black and scalding.

TROLL

OGRES

OGRES, the third species of Giants, are the least attractive and most frightening in appearance, generally having either one eye or three and a variety of other deformities. Curiously enough they are the least dangerous, for they are fantastically stupid and gullible, and are quite easily frightened. In contests with Men they are always bested; alas that their great size and terrifying, unsavory appearance is so intimidating that few Men dare to challenge them to a duel of either arms or wits. They are very susceptible to the distractions of riddles.

Ogres prefer to live in caves. Castles are second choice, and they do not like to remain outdoors overlong. They surround themselves with thorns, stones, brambles, bones, and teeth. They dress themselves after a fashion in odorous skins, the origin of which it is better not to know. Ogres have weak eyesight, flat feet, and children who are chronically adenoidal and round-shouldered.

The best Ogres have only one eye, carry a cudgel, and are very untidy with the bones.

Gnomes

GNOMES and Dwarves, now no more than distant cousins, originally came from a common ancestor. Gnomes are quite comfortable living underground, even in the kingdoms of Dwarves if not too much work is expected of them. They settle down above ground much more casually and for longer periods of time than do Dwarves, occupying themselves chiefly with mischief.

Gnomes are smaller than Dwarves and seldom grow taller than two feet. They have excessively large hands and feet at the end of spindly limbs, and affect wide leather belts in an attempt to conceal their large waistlines.

Gnomes are fun-loving and fond of practical jokes but their short tempers and irascibility do not win them many friends either among their own kind or among others. Quite often they must retreat to a solitary life in trees, caves, or forests, misunderstanding and misunderstood by all. Chattering and screeching, they plague the casual passer-by, pelting him with pine cones, stones, and turnips.

Gnomes are skilled with their hands and are useful to Tailors and Cobblers. Many of them migrate each winter far to the North, where they produce toys, puzzles, night lights, and doorstops in their likeness.

Gnomes have an unfortunate tendency to become transformed into toads; their King is particularly prone to this enchantment. Throwing water, preceded by an act of kindness, will release the Gnome. He will then feel obliged to present you with a token of value; it will usually be something edible which will enable you to understand the speech of animals or the song of birds.

It is said that Gnomes can dissolve and become invisible.

Gore, and Hazards of the Course

SPLIT tree trunks may close upon one and become prisons, distaff wounds may be curable only by centuries of sleep, wheels may be made to spin only by the feet of innocent Maidens plying the treadles. Hunting, the pleasant sport of Princes, leads to thirst and thus to drinking unwisely of enchanting pools and streams. From the Palaces of Evil Wizards fair Maids beckon across emerald lawns as, to the music of lutes and lyres and to the light of golden torches, one passes by to the safer shelter of the woodcutter's hut.

One wishing to make old bones would do well to avoid:

AGUE, suffered by soldiers sleeping in wet tents on marshes and carried to them through miasmas by mosquitoes. High fevers, cold chills, chattering teeth, raving deliriums, and blessed sweats exhaust the sufferer, who can be comforted with teas and infusions made from colicroot, sassafras bark, and quinine.

THE BLACK DEATH, which begins with the bite of infected fleas abandoning infected rats abandoning ships newly moored after a journey from a distant land. Suspect Bubonic Plague when headache and backache are followed by rigors, vomiting, lassitude, fever, and a brown tongue. Flee the Black Death when straw is spread in the streets to muffle the heavy rumble of carts laden with dead and supposed dead, if one is allowed to leave the city.

GOUT, with its red and tender swellings ap-

pearing classically in the big toe of the right foot in the small hours of the morning after a vaguely unsatisfactory evening before. Tendency to Gout is inherited, as is the irascible, strong-willed, and testy character of the sufferer, which is often accompanied by an inherited income substantial enough to afford the patient continued, if ill-advised, access to the malty liquors, strong wines, and rich meats which do so much harm. Wealth, however, can provide relief for the patient by way of a Gout stool of unsurpassed comfort, visits to spas, tenants to evict, mortgages to foreclose, and attendants to curse during the ever-recurring bouts of pain.

JAILS, and all the Fevers therein called Spotted, Putrid, Pestilential, or Typhoid. They are carried by valiant and sturdy lice through vast landscapes of dirt; overcrowded, fatigued, and starved bodies; damp straw; and stagnant puddles. Apathy, high temperature, vacant face, and a low, muttering delirium during which one plucks at rags accompanying Jail Fevers, which can persist for several weeks before death occurs.

POISONS, which may be placed in figs, apples, rings; poured into ears; administered slowly day by day or in one large dose; rubbed in the skin of slaves by experimenting Empresses or inadvertently taken by one who seeks to administer it to another. Poisons lurk beneath the covers of chalices, cling to the tips of daggers, or ripen in small crystal phials concealed among lace bosoms and wrists. Ancient and forgotten, yet still puissant, they remain on the crackling leaves of old books which invite the tongue-wetted finger of the curious.

Poisons are obtained from old Gypsy Women, Witches, and Sorceresses, or are brought in by one's Ambassador from far-off lands, or by one's Maid.

A Unicorn's horn will reveal the presence of Poisons, as will a topaz, and an adder stone, if supplied in time, will draw out poisons.

Hemlock should not be given secretly; it is an instrument of the State and should be accorded all privileges and ceremony. Its use is reserved for Philosphers and those who will not slit their wrists in warm baths.

Belladonna is given by *belle donne* to those fairer in the land so indiscreet as to reveal themselves in looking glasses. It is called Deadly Nightshade as well, under which label it is a staple of Witches.

The best Poisons are effective in small doses and have as well a long pot life.

VAPORS, a feminine affliction of the tightly laced, the overweight, the sensitive, are brought about by delicious tidbits of gossip, by shocking behavior ill suited to the drawing room, by a rush of blood to the head following an injudiciously long period of stooping in front of a keyhole.

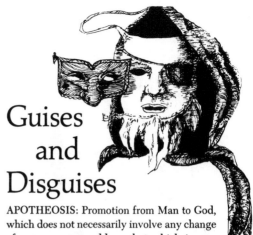

Guises and Disguises

APOTHEOSIS: Promotion from Man to God, which does not necessarily involve any change of appearance or address, but which is considered a very good thing to have happen.

INCARNATION: Assumption by a Spirit or God of the physical attributes of a Man in order that he may continue on Earth his various pursuits.

TRANSFORMATION: The complete change of substance: Man to stone, frog to Prince, swan to girl; practiced by one being on another. Wizards and Sorceresses and Gods can transform themselves without magical articles; few others can do so.

DISGUISE: Additions or subtractions to one's own appearance in order to appear other than one is: false beards, dominoes, vizards, eye patches, crutches all serve as disguises.

UNIFORMS: Clothes worn to denote one's membership in a group more devoted to work than pleasure.

COSTUMES: Clothes worn for a particular effect, for pleasure, to be temporarily other than you are.

HABITS: Sober and utilitarian garments donned to indicate a particular calling or to facilitate an immediate pursuit.

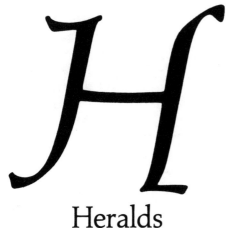

Heralds

IT is a solemn matter to appoint a Herald to your household, for he will be with you, assuming your need for him continues, forever after. His presence alone can turn a simple sandwich into a solemn banquet. Never take a Herald on a picnic.

The applicant for the post should, first of all, be eager: there are always many Heralds out of work.

He must be thoroughly familiar with the Arms of everyone you are likely to encounter, and he should be able to describe them accurately in as few words as possible.

He will keep accurate and up-to-date Rolls of Arms with pictures of the Arms on them, colored or hatched in correctly, and separate Rolls of Arms recording attendance at tournaments, battles, sieges, funerals. These Rolls will record the scores made at tournaments, the number and name of the dead and wounded in battles.

He should be able to organize and conduct a tournament, either under the direction of a Marshal or by himself. His duties include issuing invitations, crying the identity of contestants as they enter the list, starting and ending the events, and acclaiming the victors. He must not assume the role of Judge, but announce the Judge's decision clearly and promptly without opinion.

Your Herald will, in time of war, step in when the Ambassadors have stepped out. He will carry from you to the enemy messages, ultimatums, warnings, and entreaties. Unlike Ambassadors, he will always be given an audience, and promptly. By his tone of voice he should be able to evoke terror, despair, mercy, or confusion, according to the contents of your message.

Heralds expect to be consulted when new Coats of Arms are being designed. Their proper function is to inform you if the new Arms duplicate those of another person, but they seldom can refrain from voicing their opinions as to the new bearer's worthiness.

He will always wear a short tabard on which are blazoned your Arms alone, with your Badge on his hat. He may be allowed to wear spectacles.

If your household is large, with many Lords and Vassals in residence, your Herald will expect to be given the assistance of Apprentices called Poursuivants, who wear your Arms athwart their tabards. Kings and very great Lords may keep several Heralds and many Poursuivants; in this case they are well advised to appoint a King of Arms over all Heralds and Poursuivants to keep them in order.

The person of the Herald is, like that of Ambassadors and Angels, inviolate. He must not be expected to bear weapons of any sort.

Since Heralds are, after all, hired help

they must not be expected to follow you into banishment, exile, or imprisonment, nor otherwise to share your misfortune. They are free to turn their tabards inside out and seek

other employment without shame. Unlike Ambassadors, Heralds are not permitted to lie, take bribes, revel in personal publicity, or amass private fortunes in the course of their work. Therefore provision for their old age is of concern to them and it is only natural that their attendance upon you depends upon your continuing good fortune.

Hermits

HERMITS thrive and hum, do themselves very well, and generally make the best of things. They are not above having watertight roofs for their huts, or drains in their caves, and are diligent in ensuring a steady supply of honey for their table.

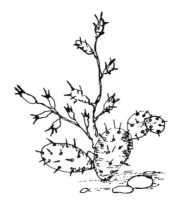

ANCHORITES show a preference for thorns, drought, and meditation. Certain that the next world will be without the above afflictions, they relish their present discomforts, which may include beds of thistles.

RECLUSES, whose major occupation is either stopping the hands of clocks or covering looking glasses with black crepe, are essentially urban and have had at one time income and property. They are found in their libraries, towers, or bedrooms mulling over a faded and fragile ballet slipper and a dried rose.

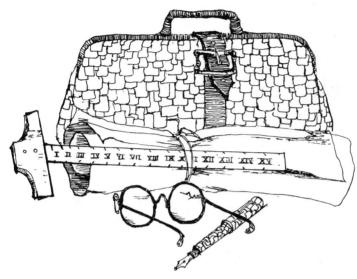

Homunculi

THESE are small men and women created by occult and magic means from exotic substances. Their creation takes place and their entire existence is spent in heavy glass jars, usually one Homunculus to a jar, surrounded by and suspended in a fluid of unknown nature, the color of which may change.

Some need feeding, some not. Occasionally a few will be clothed and crowned; others are misshapen and grotesque. Some can communicate by sign language. Records exist of Homunculi being taken for brief daily outings from their jars, but this practice may develop an appetite for the outdoors and lead to attempts to escape.

During the creation of Homunculi the jars are buried in dung heaps where the heat spontaneously given off provides constant warmth.

It is imprudent to hatch a Basilisk and mature a Homunculus in the same manure pile.

Humbugs

HUMBUGS can be told at a distance by their hats, which are slightly battered, a roll of blueprints or plans under one arm, baggy knees to their trousers, and by something to show, sell, or demonstrate to you. These may be nostrums, tonics, or specifics, but more likely they will be mechanical and scientific inventions. They are willing to sell the plans to you, and they very much hope they will work. Humbugs live in rooming houses or garrets, and are touchingly confident that one day . . .

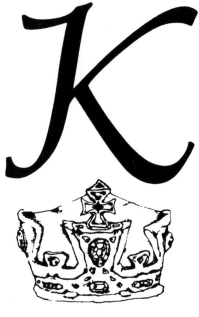

Kings

KINGS are seldom alone except in sleep, when they have dreams which influence the course of events. Even in exile there is one faithful Jester who attends them even if all others have deserted. On return from exile the single constant retainer is guaranteed meteoric promotion, which he will perhaps decline.

Kings have responsibilities to beggars' feet, and to lepers, and to those suffering King's Evil. They have Bedesmen to pray for them in return for a new gown and a few pennies each year, and Fools to teach them wisdom, and seemingly ungrateful children to plague them. Kings and Queens must have a plentiful supply of rings on hand, for they are expected to give them to those entrusted with dangerous missions and to those in charge of secret enterprises. The rings may be returned when help is needed or one's loyalty is under question, and although they are sometimes returned in unlikely ways, they are never lost. A King may have several rings out at the same time.

The titles of Kings and Emperors are long and illustrate their activities, their domains, their attributes. A King is, in his title as well as in fact, always King of some place; an Emperor is Emperor of many places, all of which are named.

Kings and Emperors may leave monuments on which great advice is graven; these will be found later, toppled but legible.

Kings may inherit little save chaos and disorderly and lawless realms, from which they create great kingdoms. Or their reigns may commence in sunlight, blessed with peace and plenty and power, and they may squander their kingdoms and end their days mad, impoverished, and alone, their lands wrested from them and divided among Barbarians.

Kings' beards may be long and gray or short and dark; it is said that some Kings do not die, but only sleep until needed.

Knights

KNIGHTS, like Kings, are anointed, and that is the end of similarity. It is possible, and indeed customary, to become a King (to say nothing of a Noble) by fact of birth. It is not possible to become a Knight without strife, difficulties, and achievement.

Begin by having yourself sent to a castle at the age of seven or eight as a Page. You will be in constant personal attendance on the Lord and Lady of the castle, waiting on them at table—although you will not yet carve or pour wine—winding yarn, carrying messages, learning sagas, songs, and tales of great deeds from the Lady, her Handmaidens, and the Chaplain. You may be taught to read and will surely have your ears boxed when necessary, but your hair will soften the blow.

At the age of fifteen you will be promoted to Squire. Expect to spend more time out of doors practicing the arts of swordplay, riding, hunting, and archery. You will learn to care for your Lord's armor and his horse. Within the castle you will be allowed to carve and pour wine at table, you will set up games after dinner and play them, you will pour your Lord's nightcap and wear silver spurs. It is permissible to fall in love with a Lady of high degree although you are expected to conceal your devotion.

Following this training you may become a Squire of the Body for two or three years—or a lifetime if you choose—attaching yourself to a Knight or Lord other than the one who has trained you. Your duties include displaying and guarding the Knight's pennon in battle, giving him your horse if he is disabled, carrying him from the field of battle if he is wounded, rescuing or ransoming him if he is captured. You will carry his armor and guard his prisoners, and provide an honorable burial if he is slain.

Those who wish to progress and become Knights may at the age of twenty or thereabouts apply to the person of a sympathetic Lord or King and present a list of suitable accomplishments. The full ceremony of Knighting is most impressive and should be experienced if at all possible. Senior Knights will attend or instruct you through the bath, the dressing in clean robes, the night-long vigil in chapel. After rest and fast in the morning, you will be led by them before the Lord conferring Knighthood and, kneeling, you will promise many good things: courage, honor, mercy, purity, kindness to your horse. The Lord will then dub you thrice on the shoulder with the flat of a sword, and per-

haps embrace you. You will be given golden spurs, a belt, and a sword. You will place "Sir" before your first name and take for surname the place from whence you came.

After choosing a Squire (optional) you will need a Task, Quest, or Cause, for it ill behooves young and able Knights to sit idle or loiter palely. Fortunately there is always an abundance of wrong to right. From time to time Knights worn by war or disappointed in love or fortune form a Brotherhood, each member adopting the same Arms and purpose. Swearing lifelong vows of mutual service and fealty, they disappear into their castle and are seldom seen thereafter except in time of strife. Their influence, however, is much felt in the world.

Knighting may be accomplished by the simple act of dubbing in situations where time is of the essence or in places where there is no tub or chapel.

You may be degraded and demoted from Knight to common citizen if you behave dishonorably or do not keep your vows. Heralds will come to you; your spurs will be hacked off, your sword belt cut off, and your sword broken. Redemption is possible, but lengthy and difficult.

Landscapes

On Moors:
    Heather, granite outcrops, storms
    Brackish, dark-watered pools
    Wild cattle, ponies, hawks
    Abandoned wells and mine shafts
    Gibbets
    Nameless men, and Robbers

HIGH PASS

CANYON

MEAD

MOOR

FOREST

SWAMP

WOOD

SPINNEY

THICKET

GLADE

GROVE

COPPICE

On Heaths:
Sand, bracken, and heather, stunted trees, flies
Peat cutters
Oblique tracks, wayside crosses
Pilgrims
Highwaymen
Corpses swinging in chains
Rabbits
Furze, broom, yarrow, bluebells

On Downs:
Groundsel, Deadly Nightshade, thistles
Chalk, grasses, beech, and fir
Wind
False horizons, earthworks, and old straight roads
Larks and lapwings
Shepherds and Quarrymen, Tinkers

In Marshes, Bogs, and Fens:
Herons, storks, terns
Preserved ships
Fleeing Clergy and Elves
Pennywort, Pimpernel, Saxifrage, and Asphodel
Bogeymen
Convicts
Cattails
Reeds, Rushes, Osiers
Will-o'-the-Wisps
Netters of fish and fowl, and their stilted huts on hummocks

In Mountains, High Passes, Canyons, Ravines, Gorges, etc.:
Returning Kings, Winds, Snow, Thorns
Falling rocks, a Shrine
Pines, Lichen, Moss
Ambush
Avalanches
Rope bridges and Landslides
A precipice and torrential river
A starving and bedraggled Army, in flight, their feet bound in rags

GORGE

CAVERN

DOWNS

VALE

DELL

HEATH

BOG

MARSH

QUAGMIRE

FEN

QUICKSAND

L

Leeches

SINCE Leeches, by contracting or expanding their bodies, can take a plump pear shape or that of an elongated worm, they are better recognized by

their color, which is olive green to brown with darker spots of the same color
their appetite for blood, which

*they draw either through a proboscis
or a three-jawed mouth which makes
a triangular bite*

To gather Leeches, wade into a pond full of them and stand still. When the part of you that is underwater is covered with them, wade out and allow the Leeches to drop off when full into the dish you have brought with you. Pulling them off mutilates the distinctive triangular scar; if you are in haste pour salt water over them and they will drop off before they are full.

It is weakening to gather too many at a time.

If preferred, you may drive a cow into the water and let the Leeches attach themselves to her. Do not use a donkey; he will not stand for it.

Fatten the Leeches on cattle blood before storing them in a pudding of clay and water. When well fed they will keep without further attention up to a year, but because they are vain they are happiest displayed in a jar in the window of an Apothecary.

There are

> *700 Leeches to a pound*
> *1,000,000 Leeches need 8 acres
> of marsh pond*
> *1 Leech will consume up to 2
> drachms of blood*
> *Allow 300 head of cattle to fat-
> ten 1,000,000 Leeches*

Leeches may be rented. For indicated use, see *Bleeding*.

Mangel-Wurzel

MANGEL-WURZEL: A type of beet which should, like all beets, be used only to feed cattle. It is a crop which seldom fails and is much planted by Serfs and Peasants.

Marquesses

MARQUESSES are ostensibly in charge of the governing of Marks and Marches, but they prefer to remain in town and over the years have abandoned this function to those whose names carry the guns: Barons.

As Marquesses, they are found in the best clubs, admirably barbered, tailored, and never far from either the weighing machine or the fireplace. They are excellent companions, always ready to chat, play cards, have drinks, and serve on committees to choose trophies. They will tell you, often without being asked, what Angostura Bitters are made of, who made Marie Antoinette's *nécessaire,* and the disastrous results of the flooding of the Neva in St. Petersburg in the winter of '87. Marquesses are interested in the results of all sporting events and play billiards themselves.

Marks and Marches

MARKS AND MARCHES: Border areas between kingdoms, dukedoms, baronies, and counties. They are the scenes of night ridings, alarums, invasions, and uprisings. There are found here outlying posts, beacons, fens, and crags on which burn flares. Rebellion and treason are hatched here, not by the population, which is tough, hardy, slightly brutal, and clad in skins if not indeed in woad, but by the Lords sent by the King to govern these desperate regions.

Merchants

MERCHANTS form Guilds in the West and Caravans in the East. They always travel in company and pride themselves on being matter-of-fact. They should be consulted when choosing a rare gift for one's betrothed, or raising a ransom for one's Liege Lord. Merchants drive hard bargains yet can often be satisfied with a grant of charter or a Court appointment for a son or daughter. Merchants are obese, have large families, and endow almshouses. They enjoy banquets of great length and hearty food, corporation politics, fine woolen and fur garments, and drink porter and Rhenish wine.

Monasteries

MONASTERIES: Places of rest and recovery from wounds or a serious setback to your Quest. Utter failures and reformed villains may take the habit and stay on permanently. Monasteries are ruled by Abbots who are either garrulous and kindly or white-maned and severe.

Monasteries are the sites of Cloisters, midnight chanting, famous rings of bells, herbs, specifics, brandied cordials, carp ponds, wholesome bread, and honey.

Myths, Fables, and Legends

MYTHS: Tales of much meaning, with no moral, rich in events and characters some say never existed. Myths never end.

FABLES: Tales for remembering when decisions are in the making, crossroads come upon, and choices to be made. They are told most unsuccessfully to children; their authors enjoy them most.

LEGENDS: Tales of the particular, wherein the true meaning and import of actions, events, and people is made clear forever.

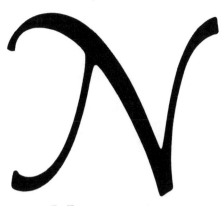

Nunneries

NUNNERIES are places of essential mystery surrounded by walled gardens of fine blooms and the most fruitful orchards in the country-side. Seek advice in Nunneries; it will be given by the Abbess, seated behind a grille in an armchair reminiscent of a throne, her skin luminous and beautiful, her hands tranquil and well manicured. The apple-cheeked and merry Novice who shows you into her presence, as well as the long-dead but not-yet-forgotten lover, are constantly remembered in the prayers of the Abbess.

Find in Nunneries vigils and visions, fasts and factions; a simple surreptitious swing may hang from the farthest apple tree and young Postulants who enjoy it are unaware that it was hung there half a century ago by the Abbess herself, who sometimes revisits it when all others are at their lacemaking.

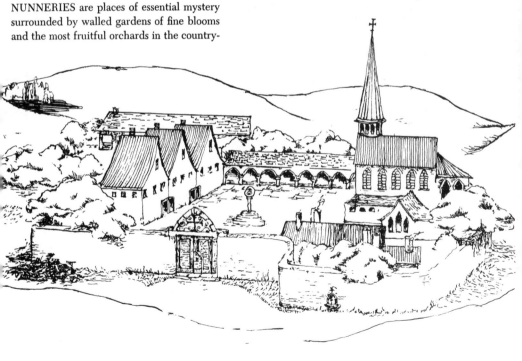

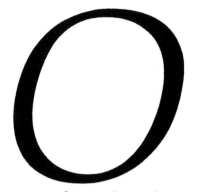

O

Offal

OFFAL: The entrails, liver, and lights of edible animals. Offal is low priced and therefore used to feed Orphans and Urchins. Offal includes tripe, fish heads and tails, plate scrapings, and garbage in general.

Oafs, Churls, Louts, and Knaves

OAFS are clumsy, bad-mannered, overweight, and have hangnails.

CHURLS are ill bred, and very likely low born in fact as well as practice. Surly of temperament and low of brow, there is no pleasure to be had from them. If they serve beer, they slop it; if they drink beer, they belch. Their points are more often than not unlaced.

LOUTS are rude, in spite of possibly good upbringing. Louts are loud, swinish, and often sent to bed without dessert. Loutishness is not necessarily permanent; it may be produced temporarily in anyone by fatigue, hunger, or frustration.

KNAVES are young Menservants who are addressed as "Ha there boy!" by Masters who do not trouble to learn their names. Knaves therefore develop a roguish, disrespectful, and troublesome character, and tend to move on to careers as minor Robbers, Footpads, or Pickpockets.

Ordeals

LANDSLIDES: The slipping of earth, rock, mud, or snow from one height to another can be an inconvenience, danger, or disaster depending on the amount of matter displaced. In any case the aftermath is characterized either by a dusty or muddy ruin.

AVALANCHES are swift, large, terrible descents of snow and ice, rock and tree, down steep precipices and mountainsides. They accompany themselves with deep, rumbling crescendos of sound which are heard afar but seldom in time to serve as warning to those in their path.

HOLOCAUSTS involve fire, and possibly wind, and are the most thoroughgoing destroyers of all, involving oast and garner, field and byre, life and limb.

CHAOS, which may result from all of the above, includes so much disorganization of so many things that the word has neither singular nor plural form.

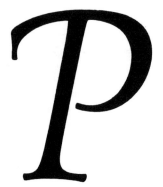

Parchment and Vellum

PARCHMENT is the skin of a sheep or goat prepared as a writing surface. It receives Edicts, Decrees, Rolls, Proclamations, Death Warrants.

VELLUM is the skin of a calf or kid prepared for the service of literature: Bibles, tomes, Books of Hours, love letters, and pardons.

Port

PORT is never kept in Carafes, for they are glass and public, meant for water and *vin ordinaire*. Port is carefully transferred instead into Decanters, which are of crystal, are intended for private tables, and hold priceless vintages. Decanters hold something worth decanting; Carafes, potations knowing no other home save the barrel.

Port may be punished, but it should never be boiled.

Boiling the Port is an atrocity committed by careless Butlers in the service of ignorant Masters. The bottle is brought up from the cellar too late to warm it slowly and properly, and is then surreptitiously placed far too close to the dining-room fire as the soup comes in. It is left there until, the distraction of the withdrawing ladies providing an opportunity for the Butler to retrieve it, it is placed on the table, overheated certainly and possibly slightly evaporated. Such Butlers, can they get way with it once, will do it every time.

Plans of battle in thin red lines on dinner tables are drawn by blue-veined fingers dipped in Port. Port is drunk by grateful grandsons of gouty grandfathers who put it down half a century before; by ailing cottagers sent down a bottle from the Hall; by two-bottle men who are helped home at dawn by cowherds from the ditch where they inadvertently spent the night or, after measuring their length on the stableyard stones, carried home on hurdles by hardy 'Ostlers.

Dregs and Lees are an unwelcome necessity found at the bottom of good bottles; the greater the wine the more bitter they are. Tasting of them occasionally may be a realistic experience, but not one to be repeated often. They are drunk by the desperate, or by Louts, or, filtered and strained, by Second Footmen.

Prince Bishops and Cardinals

PRINCE BISHOPS are dangerous men, the most puissant of all Lords Spiritual, and are adept in using the advantages of their church-

ly sanctions in addition to their temporal powers. It is considered naïve, if not dangerous,
to remind such a prelate of his calling. They
are most active during Interregnums, Regen-
cies, and the Reigns of Idiots and Dotards. A
career in the service of a Prince Bishop is
recommended for those with a scholarly bent
or a poor sword arm.

CARDINALS belong to a College and have
hats which they seldom wear. Those appointed to the Curia in Rome pass their time
in intrigue and the composition of elegant
Latin. Those outside the City are Prince
Bishops, occasionally Cadets of Princely
Houses, and are found slightly behind and to
the left of the Throne.

Princes

PRINCEHOOD is a time of waiting to become King and may be spent in adventure, danger, Quest, and victory. A Prince who lingers at Court will suffer much boredom, ill health, languor, and downright vapors. To counteract the sapping results of such inactivity they are best sent out on Quests, Grand Tours, or Hunting Expeditions. Sometimes these are taken incognito, in the company of a few friends, or one stern old adviser.

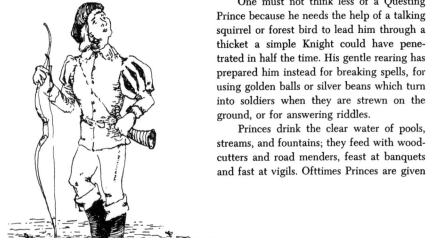

One must not think less of a Questing Prince because he needs the help of a talking squirrel or forest bird to lead him through a thicket a simple Knight could have penetrated in half the time. His gentle rearing has prepared him instead for breaking spells, for using golden balls or silver beans which turn into soldiers when they are strewn on the ground, or for answering riddles.

Princes drink the clear water of pools, streams, and fountains; they feed with woodcutters and road menders, feast at banquets and fast at vigils. Ofttimes Princes are given to cottagers to rear, or Dwarves, and reach manhood before they themselves know of their Royal birth.

Princes must learn, as did their sires, not to reveal all their plans.

Princes may be kidnapped or imprisoned none know where if their Coronation is impending. Such Princes may be impersonated by a distant cousin resembling him identically. When the Prince is released, the cousin is expected to retire gracefully.

Princes are of even temper if they are fortunate, of cheerful outlook, broad of brow and shoulder. If they seem overly demanding in insisting on marrying a real Princess it should be remembered that there are always more unmarried Princesses going to waste than other girls.

SOVEREIGN PRINCES

COUNTRIES not possessed of a King can be ruled by Princes, anointed and crowned, who make their principalities as independent and kingdomlike as possible. These Princes are eminently conscious that "Prince" means "first in place or action"; their Courts are brilliantly populated with resident Mathematicians, Composers, Astronomers, Librarians, Inventors. The palace grounds are splendid with waterworks, exotic animals, plants, and flowers, and in their gardens fly only Rare Aves.

Given, however, Evil Nature, Sovereign Princes can become very tricky and villainous as they grow older, turning into Black Princes whose brazen castles and palaces are the origin of fell deeds and abodes of terror to the countryside. In their dungeons are Dragons, at table skeletal guests, and a hundred Maidens will be found chained to spin-

ning wheels if they have not indeed suffered a worse fate. Sovereign Princes may take up magic and end among the ranks of Evil Wizards and Arch-Warlocks.

Sovereign Princes will be large-boned and heavily muscled, of dark mien, and clad in red or black armor. They will be found scouring the countryside, laying waste, and collecting exorbitant taxes, first-born babes, and the lands of others.

Princesses

KINGS have either one daughter, three, seven, or twelve. If more than one, each will be more beautiful than the next, or uglier than the next. Or all will be ugly save one, who will be the fairest in the land. Princesses are hard on shoe leather, Maids, Ladies in Waiting, and each other. They are subject to Evil Stepmothers, Witches who have been offended at their Christenings, and imprisonment in towers. (Dungeons are seemingly reserved for Princes.)

Given unsavory tasks to do, such as kissing toads or serving in disguise as Scullery Maids or Goosegirls, they generally do very well, but they are seldom adept at spinning.

During a dearth of Princes a Princess must perforce sit and mope, companioned by a pet goldfish or songbird, unless her father has married her or betrothed her during infancy to some ancient King. Few Princesses have the experience or initiative to search through sleet and hail for the castle of the neighboring Prince; most set three tasks for suitors when they do at last appear.

Princesses have hands which can be given as a reward for the head of an enemy.

Queens

IF they do not expire in childbirth or at the hands of the Headsman, Queens tend to endure. By and large they make very good wives and, even if only Consorts, are quite competent to rule kingdoms in the absence of their husbands.

Queens are advised by Prince Bishops and Cardinals, attended and flattered by their Courts, kept informed by Ladies in Waiting and their own Spies, are spied upon by the same, and are sometimes supplanted by an ambitious Maid of Honor. Queens can trust their Confessors, and certainly their old Nurses, who will wait each night till revels' end to unlace the stiff lace gowns and put away the jewels.

If they are Queens Regnant they concern themselves with expeditions and explorers, ecclesiastics and economics; if Consort, with the gentle concerns of their daughters and sons, endeavoring to instill in them industry and honor. Seldom rash, more often giddy, their extravagances may evoke inquiries into the Household Exchequer.

A Queen Consort in time of war may accompany her husband in battle, and in any case seldom fails to embroider his standard and gloves with her own hands.

Queens travel well, and often.

They are accomplished needlewomen, although they do not make lace, and are expected to be highly devout. Their amusements include *tableaux vivants,* cards, hunting, and masked balls.

Quicksand

QUICKSAND is a fate befalling the otherwise unpunishable or uncatchable. A cold, wet, nocturnal death, it is best suffered in the presence of a witness who may or may not affect to extricate you from it. Find quicksand where water seeps, flows, or bubbles underneath sand; it is treacherous, movable, and detectable only at great risk.

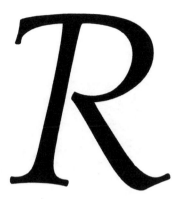

Ransom

IF captured in battle, Ransom above and beyond horse and armor must be paid. While it is being collected from the Serfs and Peasants of your fief, or the subjects of your kingdom, you must expect to languish either in a high tower or in a dark dungeon. If the Ransom asked is large it may take years to amass; much time can pass also if your holdings are small and money hard to come by.

Your Lady will of course divest herself of her jewels right away; Moneylenders may demand exceedingly high interest or special privileges they could not otherwise attain. Your captors may also haggle over lands and boundaries or raise the amount of Ransom, but they will likely be aware that such practices are in bad taste.

As negotiations and arrangements proceed, your time can be passed in song, composing poetry, scratching your name or the numbers of days passed on the stone walls of your prison. A small bird may become your companion, or a mouse enliven your solitude.

109

Returning home at last, you will seem to have increased in value and to shine with a special light for a time.

Sanctuary

SANCTUARY is sought at the very last, when all other alternatives have bewilderingly closed or been exhausted. It is the inevitable goal of betrayed and landless Kings, of abandoned or widowed Queens, of petty Thieves, seditious Barons, escaped Convicts.

The way to Sanctuary is pointed by roadside crosses which cannot be confused with milestones or shrines even though they are seen but dimly in the dark of the moon. Churches offering Sanctuary set limits on the safe area: it may begin generously thirty paces from the church door, or when a special knocker has been sounded, or only when within the choir stall or seated on a small stool. Priests will attempt, perhaps perfunctorily, to persuade you to give yourself up; you will be requested to leave your arms without and, after confession, to don the habit of the order and eat with the Brothers, spreading no scandal and plotting no treason.

In some cases having reached and enjoyed Sanctuary then entitles you to leave the realm without being molested, but only if you assume the posture of poverty, quit the country swiftly and by foot, and swear not to return without the King's pardon.

Sepulture

CRYPTS, underground and vaulted chambers beneath the altars of churches, hold stone Sarcophagi containing Heroes, Martyrs, Maidens, Kings, and Queens, whose effigies are carved in great and serene detail upon the lid. Crypts in private houses are much used for secret rites, as storerooms for wine butts, and as housing for Giants, Dragons, and Madwomen.

Sepulchres, ghostly white, loom among the cypress trees of cemeteries and contain the caskets of ancient families.

Barrows, Tumuli, and Cairns hold chambers which provide habitation for the dead Warriors therein who, seated with their weapons at hand, await one last sound of a horn. The neighborhood of Barrows is restless and best avoided at dusk.

Catacombs are for Martyrs, wrapped in linen. Pyres are for individual Warriors, their ships, and horses.

Felons are buried summarily in the prison yard, and Paupers behind the parish house, both in simple coffins without caskets.

Kings, if they are not entombed in Sarcophagi or Mausoleums, will rest beneath cathedral floors, or in a Barrow en masse with their armies. Their hearts may be placed in urns and given to one place, their heads to another, and their bodies to yet another.

Burial by night, or in secret, is suspect. Disinterments, however, if properly authorized, should take place under precisely these conditions. Those not properly authorized generally do.

Gravediggers feel entitled to coffin handles and hinges if they are of value, and particularly to the nails of Murderers' coffins, which they sell as souvenirs.

Suicides' graves should be at crossroads, pointing north and south, but the graves of all others should allow the head to rest in the west and look east.

The drowned, or otherwise unrecoverable, may be remembered by mighty Cenotaphs rather than graves.

111

Serfs
and
Peasants

IF at times Serfs and Peasants seem sour, dour, and poor, it may be that their diet of black bread, small beer, and green cheese disagrees with them. All are expected to be loyal, prudent, strong, patient, ruddy-cheeked, low-browed, strong-ankled, good husbandmen, merry at harvest, and contrite at Mass.

With knuckled forelock and cheek-couched tongue they give tithes, dimes, corvées, scutage; they contribute to their Lord's ransom, to his son's coming-of-age present; they pay to use his mill, press, pas-

turage, ovens; they drain marshes, plow fields, mend roads, and provide their Lord with his profession of organizing his countryside to the greatest economic and political advantage. Some Lords are uncertain as to what comprises "advantage," or have ideas of their own, or expect the advantage to be all to them and not at all to the countryside. By and large, however, the Lord is expected to protect his people from invasion, civil strife, flood and famine, from the intrusion of other Lords, and from his own worst nature.

Peasants pay in money for the land they hold; Serfs pay in time and produce for the land which holds them. All present their peti-

fore curfew they tell ghost stories around the light of tallow dips and rushlights.

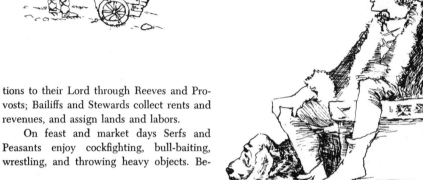

tions to their Lord through Reeves and Provosts; Bailiffs and Stewards collect rents and revenues, and assign lands and labors.

On feast and market days Serfs and Peasants enjoy cockfighting, bull-baiting, wrestling, and throwing heavy objects. Be-

113

Sorceresses

SORCERESSES, when they are tall, beautiful, grave, and clad in flowing robes, are oft confused with Elves or Fairy Queens.

When they are ancient, stooped, and shawled, they are thought to be Witches.

Sorceresses are neither.

Sorceresses are the opposite of Witches, as Wizards are to Warlocks. They share with Wizards the same burning ambition to bend things to their will, be it good or evil. To this end they, like Wizards, assemble their own batteries of crafts, arts, skills, and magic. Unlike Witches, they are their own mistresses and the choice of good or evil is theirs. Unlike Elves or Fairies, they are mortal, though long-lived.

A heavy veil hangs over much of the world of Sorceresses, perhaps by their intention. They choose their Serving Maids and Page Boys from those who can keep themselves to themselves, and they travel less than Wizards. Their abodes are in obscure places and their pursuits are personal and not political.

Sorceresses wait, and receive those who come to them. Seek them in glades and groves. Their homes may be open, airy, furnished austerely with an ivory chair on a dais and a golden tripod. Or they may be modest huts with a three-legged stool and a cauldron, yet the seat of great wisdom. Sorceresses specialize in divining, foretelling, and advising; they are mistresses of all magic and particularly in the use of water, fine sand, and crystal orbs.

Spirits, Demons, and Ghosts

THERE are more Spirits than we know of, and some we do know of cannot be named. Some may be laid to rest, others were never alive and are thus immortal. There are Spirits summonable, and some are biddable when they have arrived. Some darken the face of the Sun, some guard but do not possess material things.

SPIRITS

There are Spirits to whom time and space do not exist. They travel swiftly, circling and girdling the earth in the twinkling of an eye, always to a purpose. These Spirits are sent or summoned, and they must be allowed to depart when their tasks are accomplished. Djinns and Afrits may live in pots or bottles or lamps. These receptacles, the prisons to which they have been confined by trickery or for their misdeeds, can be found at the bottom of the sea, from whence they are recovered in the much-mended nets of poor Fishermen. Once released, the Spirits therein, like the newly hatched chick to its shell, are very difficult if not indeed impossible to reconfine. They expect to be made to perform a service or services in return for their freedom.

There are place Spirits who guard and govern groves, waters, mountains, and all the things therein. To harm them or their domains is unwise, for they are more puissant than you. They are also watched over by greater Spirits.

Needing no habitation save air, the random and restless Spirits summonable by magic are occupied in assisting or opposing the Spirits named Demons whose habitation is Hell.

Some Spirits lead astray, and some lead home. Spirits can appear at will in any form, animal or human.

Apparitions exist, cannot be exorcised since they were never real people, and are mostly found out of doors.

Phantoms and Specters are the creations of magic and are not true Spirits; they are usually temporary and are intended to baffle, confuse, and distract you.

There are Will-o'-the-Wisps; it is dangerous to follow these *Ignes Fatui*, for the path through the misty marshes will lead you to quicksand.

There are Leprechauns; it is useless to follow them, for they will not lead you to the gold.

There are Banshees, Doppelgangers, and Revenants. Do not look or listen; they presage your death.

117

DEMONS

OF Demons there is good reason for terror. Sent forth from Hell in the company of Lords of Darkness who are Fallen Angels—Devils who are emanations and multiplications of The Devil—Demons are troops picked instructions to Familiars, preside at Sabbats and Esbats, and assist the efforts of their fellow Demons and mortal Evil-Doers whose aspirations are in line with The Devil's aim of corruption, havoc, and swelling the population of Hell.

All may assume human or animal forms at will. The most popular choice is that of a

from the ranks of dead Witches and Warlocks.

Called at any hour from their brief and painful rest on fiery pallets, these Demons issue from the Gates of Hell charged with tasks at which they dare not fail. They must recruit more Witches and Warlocks, report on backsliders and malingerers among The Devil's earthly ranks, deliver messages and dark Man; the most dangerous, that of an Angel. They are masters of all forms of Man and beast, the costumes of all countries, and all tongues, yet they have difficulty disguising their cloven hooves.

Demons are plagued with fevers, itches, ulcers, boils, blisters, and hoof-and-mouth disease.

Incubi and Succubi, handsome and beautiful beyond earthly expectation, sit on the chests of sleepers and give them fearful, morbid, and baroque dreams which are intended to seduce the sleeper into The Devil's service.

Rushed, hurried, pursued by their own Demons threatening punishment should they fail, these Demons suffer not the worst lot. There are Demons whose existence is more mean and wretched: those who man and staff Hell itself. They are the souls of less gifted Witches and Warlocks and the souls of the miscellaneous who have before death profited in some way from traffic with The Devil.

To these fall the tasks of stoking the great infernos, maintaining the engines of torture, roasting, flailing, melting, liquifying the damned.

Their Familiars desert them at the Gates of Hell; friendless they descend and friendless remain to the end of Eternity. Their human form is taken from them and replaced by misshapen, grotesque, pain-wracked bodies furnished only with knotted and tortured muscles scarce equal to the labors they must perform. Limbs grow from awkward places, as does hair and scales; they are patched with heavy, rank fur

which renews itself constantly as the flames singe it off. None have eyelids, for they cannot sleep; if the tongues are left in their mouths it is only in order that they may be parched, cracked, and bitten. Bare of back for the Overseer's flail should they falter or pause for a moment in their tasks, they descend to their labors which will never end. There is no electricity in Hell.

Amid the fumes, brazen rivers, glowing coals, raging flames, and afflicting ashes they toil, their suffering indistinguishable from those they are causing to suffer. Who is to say which agony is the greater—that of being forever tortured or that of forever torturing? If there is no rest or peace for the body on the rack or immersed in boiling oil, there is no rest for the Demon manning the rack or keeping the oil at seethe. Recall the life of Witches and Warlocks on Earth—their love of sloth, fondness of ease, lack of willingness to work—then pity their life in Hell. There they have not even a pallet of ashes; they are nurtured on cinders and pitch where before they supped, albeit with a long spoon, on loaves and ale. And where before they assembled with their own kind for dark revels, in Hell there is no speech save curses and shrieks.

GHOSTS

GHOSTS are those whose bodies are dead but whose spirits have not used up their life. They express themselves in many ways:

a sense of creeping cold
dim or skeletal outlines
a wisp of song
moans, sighs, groans, expres-
sions of misery, pain
bitter weeping
dragging chains
a candle blown out

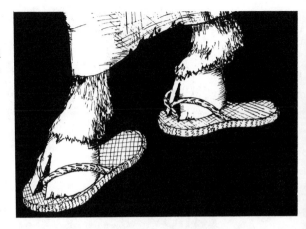

Animals will sense the presence of a Ghost first; Owls may announce them by hooting.

Like fine wines, Ghosts do not travel well. It is their custom to live near the place where they died, preferably an ancient and fine house built over or near the ruins of a previous and more melancholy dwelling. Within the house itself they show a fondness for a particular bedroom, battlement, staircase.

They appear gradually and are sometimes not believed at first. The presence of a Ghost evokes the presence of a friend as well: the Lawyer, the Doctor, the Priest. In their company it is well to determine what it is the Ghost wants.

It may want to be let in, or let out. It may want a proper burial, an old injustice corrected, a proper heir restored, a treasure found and returned, a Murderer brought to trial. When this is accomplished the Ghost will be seen no more on Earth.

Ghosts demand all of one's attention and if they don't get it they go away. They dislike laughter and ridicule, and are not likely to appear before skeptics, those who look upon them as a nuisance or just another mouth to feed, Doctors who think their patients are suffering from brain fever, and Housekeepers.

Ghosts do not live forever.

Companies of Ghosts who cannot rest because of some unexpiated sin or treason may upon occasions of great need be summoned en masse by horn.

See *Exorcism.*

123

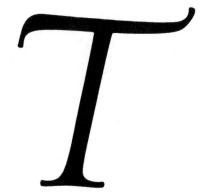

Tallow and Wax

TALLOW: Animal fat, used for smearing wounds, greasing cart wheels and burning in dips.

WAX: From bees and plants, used for seals, for candles, for small images for Witches to stick thorns in.

Tinkers and Peddlers

TINKERS and Peddlers are seemingly involved in selling ribbons and odds and ends of finery, usually reconditioned, at fairs and in the courtyards of castles, or in sharpening knives, mending china, retinning pots and pans, and repairing scissors. Unlike Merchants proper, they are solitary men of no fixed abode, lean men with eyes shifty and darting, and often a trace of Gypsy blood; it is well to give them audience, for the bauble they offer at an exorbitant price may conceal a message of great importance. The Tinker's tall, wide-brimmed hat and eye patch make him an excellent cover for a Wizard in disguise. Tinkers are often in trouble with the law; some have had their ears notched or cheeks branded, in which case they most certainly will not be Wizards incognito. Tinkers have histories, and know those of others. If come upon in the woods, they offer hospitality.

Young Ladies will be well advised not to leave their Serving Wenches long in a Tinker's company, for he will almost certainly run away with one of them. Tinkers pass their nights on heaths, in hovels, or warming their hands before the brazier of the castle guardroom. They have a lean dog, and sometimes a cart or a caravan.

Torture, Punishment, and Execution

THOUGH the means are often the same, the intents of Torture, Punishment, and Execution differ.

Torture takes place, and quite properly, privately, below ground, in the dark presence of the Torturer, a Scribe to record the answers you are expected to give, and a Questioner. Torture is intended to extract information in order that one may be punished, especially where confessions do not flow freely.

Punishment is most often public, lit by the sun, occupying a square or hilltop, and attended by throngs if not indeed by multitudes. Punishment is expected to elicit re-

morse, and good resolutions, to provide an example to the community, and, especially in the case of Executions, to ensure that you will not commit the same crime or indeed any other crime again.

In neither case does the one who asks the questions or imposes the sentence turn the wheel or wield the axe.

Torturers feel neither heat nor cold and have no other occupation. They may be deaf, or have their tongues cut out, and are curiously swarthy for men who spend so much of their time in the dark. Torturers reek of mutton, rust, and cold sweat.

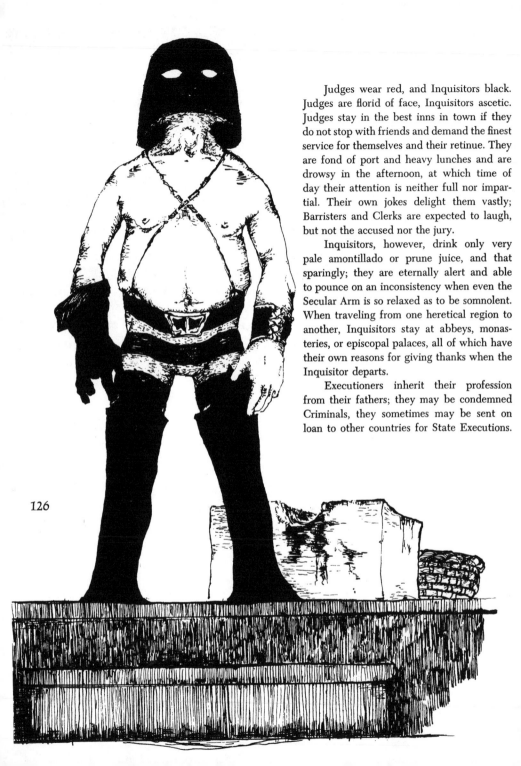

Judges wear red, and Inquisitors black. Judges are florid of face, Inquisitors ascetic. Judges stay in the best inns in town if they do not stop with friends and demand the finest service for themselves and their retinue. They are fond of port and heavy lunches and are drowsy in the afternoon, at which time of day their attention is neither full nor impartial. Their own jokes delight them vastly; Barristers and Clerks are expected to laugh, but not the accused nor the jury.

Inquisitors, however, drink only very pale amontillado or prune juice, and that sparingly; they are eternally alert and able to pounce on an inconsistency when even the Secular Arm is so relaxed as to be somnolent. When traveling from one heretical region to another, Inquisitors stay at abbeys, monasteries, or episcopal palaces, all of which have their own reasons for giving thanks when the Inquisitor departs.

Executioners inherit their profession from their fathers; they may be condemned Criminals, they sometimes may be sent on loan to other countries for State Executions.

126

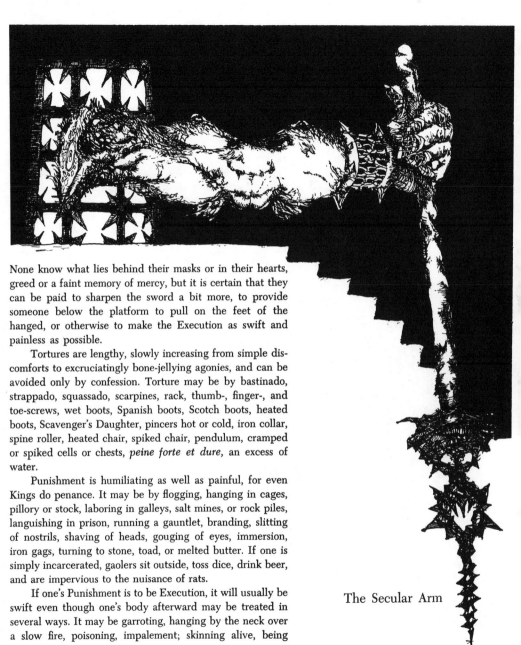

None know what lies behind their masks or in their hearts, greed or a faint memory of mercy, but it is certain that they can be paid to sharpen the sword a bit more, to provide someone below the platform to pull on the feet of the hanged, or otherwise to make the Execution as swift and painless as possible.

Tortures are lengthy, slowly increasing from simple discomforts to excruciatingly bone-jellying agonies, and can be avoided only by confession. Torture may be by bastinado, strappado, squassado, scarpines, rack, thumb-, finger-, and toe-screws, wet boots, Spanish boots, Scotch boots, heated boots, Scavenger's Daughter, pincers hot or cold, iron collar, spine roller, heated chair, spiked chair, pendulum, cramped or spiked cells or chests, *peine forte et dure,* an excess of water.

Punishment is humiliating as well as painful, for even Kings do penance. It may be by flogging, hanging in cages, pillory or stock, laboring in galleys, salt mines, or rock piles, languishing in prison, running a gauntlet, branding, slitting of nostrils, shaving of heads, gouging of eyes, immersion, iron gags, turning to stone, toad, or melted butter. If one is simply incarcerated, gaolers sit outside, toss dice, drink beer, and are impervious to the nuisance of rats.

If one's Punishment is to be Execution, it will usually be swift even though one's body afterward may be treated in several ways. It may be garroting, hanging by the neck over a slow fire, poisoning, impalement; skinning alive, being

The Secular Arm

sealed in a spiked barrel and rolled down a street, or being sewn in a bag with dogs or vipers; boiling alive, precipitation from rocks, simple hanging, or beheading.

AUTOS-DA-FE have privileges and perquisites attached to them on which you should insist. You are entitled to be accompanied to the stake, which should be at the top of a hill, by lines of black-robed Clergy wearing pointed hoods and masks. You must be provided with a ragged robe and a chain around your neck and wrists, and have bare feet.

Carts must be provided for Heretics, and their hands should be chained to the cart in front of them.

Tumbrils are for Aristocrats on their way to the guillotine, and their hands should be tied behind their backs with rope.

Knouts are for Peasants

129

Cats are for Sailors

Flails are for Serfs

Horsewhips are for Dastards

Truncheons are for drubbings given to Unruly Mobs

Axes are for beheading Commoners

Whips are for Galley Slaves

Swords are for beheading Traitors

Imported Headsmen are a courtesy accorded condemned Royalty

Fines are for the Fortunate

Confiscation is for the Condemned

GALLOWS are the formal framework from which justice depends. Gallows are public, within a large square or topping an easily accessible hill, and may accommodate several ropes at a time. There will be a trap door for friends of the hanged to pull smartly on the feet of the departing, hastening his journey. The way to the Gallows, long or short, is thronged with spectators; they will hand the condemned much drink and good advice on the way; he should toss back the empty tankards with jokes, wit, and cheer. The custom of tipping the Hangman is considered by many to be excessive and not to be encouraged. Bodies of the hanged may be displayed afterward for the remainder of the day, or cut down and taken away for burial forthwith.

GIBBETS are for rough, solitary justice for the lesser Criminals—Highwaymen, Poachers, Horse Thieves. They are found at crossroads and accommodate one at a time. Mandrakes flourish beneath, nourished on the juices and dropping gobbets of flesh from the body, which is left to rot in chains as a warning to passers-by.

Tournaments

THE occasions for Tournaments, or Tourneys, are pleasant: summertime, weddings, coronations, comings of age, entertainment for visitors of importance. They give occasion for omnipresent Ladies to display new gowns, and the castle to display new flags and banners and pennants, for Knights to display their skill, and horses their new caparisons, for Heralds to display their knowledge of Arms, and Judges their wisdom. Beggars display their afflictions and their empty almsbowls, Jugglers and Magicians their magic, Pickpockets their agility, Peddlers their wares, and, as always, small boys their ability to carry bucket after bucket of water to the horses, even though admission is free.

Tournaments are composed of Jousts,

one-to-one contests of two riders, charging at each other from opposite directions with lance, sword, mace, or spear. If a wooden, straw, or cloth barrier is placed between the opponents the contest is called a Tilt.

The Melee, the main event, is saved until the last, when all able-bodied contestants left from previous Jousts or Tilts form into two teams, enclose themselves within the confines of the List, and engage in hand-to-hand, horse-to-horse combat until all are disabled or the Judge or Marshal, through the services of a Herald, stops the fracas at the end of the day. There follows a banquet.

When giving a Tournament, provide a List one quarter longer than it is wide, with stout barriers enclosing it. Cover the ground with straw to cushion the fallen, and cover the gallery for the Ladies with gay awnings against the sun. Allow visiting and resident Heralds ample time off to compare notes, bring their Rolls of Arms up to date, and gossip.

It is prudent to obtain permission of the King to hold a Tournament, for Kings are ofttimes uncertain as to if a Tournament is only a cover for plotting treachery by large groups of magnificently armed and horsed Nobles. If the King's presence is sought, or at least his blessing, it will do much to allay undue suspicion.

Ladies are expected to provide themselves with ample ribbons, laces, scarves, gloves, and flowers to bestow as favors beforehand on their chosen champions. A Queen of Joy, or Love, or Beauty must be chosen from among them; it is she who will bestow upon the victor the golden arrow, the silver buckle, or the silken banner at the close of day.

Trollops, Trulls, Bawds, Doxies, and Strumpets

TROLLOPS, TRULLS, BAWDS, DOXIES, STRUMPETS: Ladies whose company, which is secured and enhanced by a glass or two of gin, is obtainable at any city tavern though not so often at a country inn. Loud of voice, untidy in speech, and disheveled in appearance, they may be either in league with a Footpad or warn you of one lying in wait for you. Their little brothers are Cutpurses, their older brothers Gallows Birds.

Trudge

TRUDGE: The slow, weary, yet determined walk of one who has no alternative but to continue.

Trysts, Rendezvous, and Assignations

TRYSTS are best kept in bowers, glades, or arbors. Rendezvous, the subsequent Trysts, in places which hold tender memories, the scent of flowers, and moonlight. If they are for saying farewell, keep them in a bower at dawn if the farewell is temporary; under a lurid sunset at crossroads if the farewell is permanent.

Assignations are properly arranged through a friend, maid, or valet and take place at dusk or after in an abandoned barn or mill. They may be kept by someone other than the one you had expected to find, or by someone who had other ideas in mind than yours. They are sometimes a trap, and whatever the outcome one is seldom the same afterward.

Vampires

VAMPIRES are to bodies what Ghosts are to Spirits: restless, unexpired, and needful. The Vampire possesses a body which must be clothed, housed, and fed in unique ways.

A Vampire may be recognized by the following characteristics:

He possesses an unnatural pallor, full red lips, red fires in his eyes, long, pointed canine teeth, hairy palms of hands, curving yellowish fingernails clotted with blood, and fetid breath particularly rank and corrupt.

Before feeding, a Vampire is markedly lean and gaunt. Pallor is noticeable although the lips and eyes are at all times sanguine. The skin is cold and dry. If he possesses a beard or moustache it will be faded and somewhat thinned.

After feeding, the gauntness and pallor are replaced by substantial bloat and engorgement of the entire body, the skin becoming mottled red, moist, and warm. Hair and beard will become rejuvenated, and there will be marked succulence of the lips.

Vampires are prone to dark red hair; blond Vampires are extremely rare, and bald ones almost unheard of.

If a Vampire is encountered in his coffin, he will be bloodstained about the mouth, chin, and chest as well as under the fingernails. If a vein is opened, blood will gush forth hotly; his eyes will be open at all times.

Vampires observe a strict etiquette and a technique more complex and almost more predictable than that of most night creatures.

Vampires arise from their grave, tomb, or coffin at nightfall as hunger dictates and must return there at first cockcrow. When traveling, which unsettled political conditions force them to do from time to time, they must provide themselves with a coffin or earth box containing their native soil and may cross water only when in the box, and then at great peril.

Upon arising they may assume the form of a mist, either red or white, a bat, a rodent, a dog, or they may prefer to retain their own form. Vampires can pass through doors, windows, walls, and other barriers to gain access to their victims.

When a Vampire reaches his victim he must, if the victim is a new one, be invited in the first time. For this reason they prefer as victims those who were near and dear to them in life, for the chances of receiving this crucial initial invitation are better.[*]

To quiet victims Vampires can practice mesmerism, promise immortality, or use great force. They prefer to return to the same victim time after time, sucking blood in increas-

[*] In no case can they come in without finding an opening themselves or mesmerizing you into providing one. They cannot, for instance, transform themselves into a bat, hide in a delivery basket, and effect entry that way.

Before and After Feeding

135

ing draughts until the victim has passed through exhaustion, anemia, dessication, and death.

Vampires do not molest each other, nor do they take nourishment from Ghouls.

To become a Vampire, the following steps may be taken:

1. *Be born as the offspring of a Witch and The Devil. This is not necessary but it is said to be very helpful.*

2. *Lead during life a career of more than ordinary wickedness, dissolution, and sin. Delight in all foul, gross, and selfish passions, and practice Black Magic.*

3. *Be a Werewolf toward the end of life, for this will give you contact with Vampires and you can then ask one yourself how to proceed further.*

4. *Live in a Slavonic country. They possess the highest ratio of Vampires to people and the odds are therefore greater that you will become one. Also, there is an excellent chance you will be bitten by a Vampire and if this happens often enough you will automatically become a Vampire after death.*

5. *Die excommunicated from the Church, if possible by suicide.*

6. *See to it that you are buried, with mutilated rites, in desecrated ground.*

Vampires cannot pass by crossroads swiftly; the choice of roads puzzles them and they must pause there until dawn, when they are obliged to return to their graves.

Yet this dilemma does not prevent them from attacking passers-by.

Nor is the Vampire proof against garlic; all forms and parts of this plant cause him to pale, snarl, and retreat. Crosses, church bells, persons born on Saturday, a piece of consecrated Host, and mustard seeds defeat his purpose.

Vampires do not reflect in mirrors. Dogs fear them. Coaches are sometimes driven by Vampires, but the horses dislike it.

Destruction of a Vampire cannot be accomplished by simple exorcism. More drastic action is called for:

Find the Vampire in his coffin.
Cut off his head.
Drive a stake, preferably of ash, through his heart.
Burn the head and body.
Bury the ashes at a crossroads, under a cairn of stones.

Female Vampires are less common than male but are equally dangerous. They may be found at times situated in a town house of impeccable address and themselves possessed of a robust and compelling beauty which establishes them swiftly as Reigning Toasts. These assets, together with an income of proportion generous enough to offset its dubious origin, enable them to constantly replenish their following of Guardsmen, Dandies, and Beaux. These gentlemen, who come to regard the lady with growing unease as their comrades disappear, seldom expose her publicly but are relieved when one less gentlemanly than they applies the necessary remedies.

Female Vampires, if they are less brilliant, independent, and vigorous, may be kept semienslaved in the vast and webbed crypts of expert male Vampires. In groups of three or seven they affect chiffon, pallor, and sleep-walking.

Viscounts and Baronets

VISCOUNTS AND BARONETS are known best by their number (the seventh, the second, the eleventh), for theirs are the most hereditary titles of all. Of all the Peerage they are the least war-going, disputatious, or belligerent and thus are not subject to the heir-sapping hazards of war. Dueling accounts for most violent deaths among Baronets and they are prudent enough to leave a son behind to carry on the title.

Foppish in youth and spry and dapper in old age, with admirable moustaches, Baronets and Viscounts are urban coves, found much in clubs, governments, and at the best dinner tables.

Wands, Staffs, and Rods

WANDS are the shortest of the lot, and are not long enough to reach the floor. If of wood, the Wand is peeled. They may be decorated and tipped with a significant finial. If used for diving they may be forked. With a Wand, wave and waft.

STAFFS are stout, for leaning on, for giving drubbings, and for Patriarchs to use in lieu of a sceptre.

RODS are rather more slender, but inflexible, and are used for administering occasional whippings, smiting, and adorning ceremonies.

Werewolves

THEY are never quite Wolves. Even at the peak of their transformation they retain many of the features of Men. Werewolves are hollow-eyed, burning of skin, with fangs protruding from the lower lip. They travel alternately on all fours and on hind feet; their legs are calloused and scabbed. Hair will be found on the palms of their hands and on the soles of their feet. The longer they continue their foul practice the less difference there is between the one guise and the other.

Werewolves eat the flesh of living humans, preferring children to all other things. They have at all times a raging thirst, but do not drink blood. Weapons and tools, other than their claws or fangs, are useless to them. Werewolves tire easily and cannot retain the form of Wolf beyond daybreak.

If wounded in the guise of Wolf the body of the Man will bear the scar as well. When a Werewolf is killed he changes at death back into a Man.

137

Exorcism is of dubious benefit against Werewolves. Use the same precautions as for Vampires.

Werewolves are of two sorts: voluntary and involuntary. Those who have been bitten once too often by a Vampire, or have been cursed into Werewolfdom by a malevolent Witch, or have inadvertently placed themselves in the hands of an evil or incompetent experimenter with youth-giving elixirs and potions are all involuntary Werewolves. They have little or no control over their changes from Man to Wolf and Wolf to Man, and are subject to Phases of the Moon.

Those who wish to be Werewolves for pleasure may become so by obtaining from a Witch or Sorceress a salve which, when rubbed well into the skin, will turn one into a Wolf and back again. The salve may well be habit-forming; the idle experimenter may well find that it is not possible to be a truly voluntary Werewolf for long.

Werewolves are most frequently come upon:

> *in February*
> *during the full moon*
> *in the countryside*
> *at night*
> *traveling in packs*

Witches and Warlocks

WHEN famine stalks the land and times are not favorable or generous to the unemployed and unskilled, those who are ambitious, greedy, and ill disposed to work can become Witches and Warlocks, thus providing themselves with easy sustenance and livelihood.

All that is needed is that the Witch- or Warlock-to-be enter into a Pact with The Devil. The conditions of the Pact vary from individual to individual, but from time beyond record the following constants have figured largely in Pacts.

The Devil gets You; for your lifetime you are bound to the befuddlement and destruction of Good, and after your death he gains possession of your soul and its services forever after in Hell.

You get:

Knowledge of and power to practice magic for the dismay, discomfort, and destruction of Men and their good works. Included among your Powers are:

> *invisibility*
> *souring milk in pans*
> *summoning storms*
> *transforming self and others*
> *wrecking ships*
> *potioning, poisoning, blasting*
> *blistering, blighting*
> *cursing (both Solemn and Casual)*
> *curing, divining*
> *animating the inanimate*
> *transvecting*

Possession of a Familiar, whose presence makes the above Powers possible. The Familiar, a Demon from Hell whose material body will be that of a

> *toad*
> *turtle*
> *louse*
> *flea*
> *cat*
> *bat*
> *bedbug*
> *cockroach*
> *beetle*

or other domestic animal, has been instructed and empowered by The Devil to coach and assist you in the practice of magic. He will see to it that you remember your side of the Pact and exhort you always to be totally Evil; it will be he who informs on you if you are not. If you forget while brewing up a potion what is the next ingredient or procedure, he will tell you, for he alone is entrusted with the key to the Book of Lore, or Grimoire. It is he who, if through carelessness or disinclination you pass up a chance to attend a wedding or Christening and make mischief, will see that you attend.

You will not be able to fortell and divine without him.

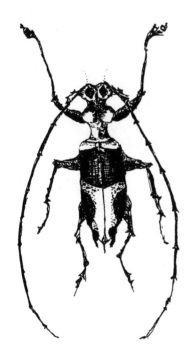

Membership in a Coven, which will be composed of twelve Witches and/or Warlocks, their Familiars, and one Officer. Covens exist to provide social life and instruction in community disservice, and assemble at Sabbats and Esbats.

Protection from discovery, exposure, foreclosure, poverty, ill health, malice of other Witches and Warlocks, the justice of Men, and other misfortunes nameable by you at the time the Pact is made. Inexhaustible wealth and long and vigorous life are the most common demands made of The Devil, and he readily agrees to these at the time since he has no intention of keeping faith with this clause. There are few Witches and Warlocks who are young, healthy, attractive, and rich, and of those who are, a large number are Wizards or Sorceresses, not Witches or Warlocks at all.

On the matter of Transformation, the more beautiful a Witch's or Evil Sorceress's Transformation, the more repellent and hideous you will find her true form underneath. Thus, a Witch who appears as young, desirable, comely, possessed of all good fortune and splendid habitation is not truly so. The outward appearances of splendor and success either are a recruiting device of The Devil or a necessity for the Witches and Warlocks, whose base and evil lives are often so foul that they lose their human forms altogether and must assume such Transformations in order to function in the human world. But to them their silken robes are hair shirts, the jewels and baubles which dazzle our eyes are rusty chains, and each forkful of dainty confection turns in their mouths to Mangel-Wurzel gruel, which is all their sole, decaying tooth can manage.

143

Pacts with The Devil have been made for limited times—seven years, fourteen years, thirty years—after which time the Witch or Warlock is to be released from all obligation and can make away with the profits of the venture. However, Witchcraft is habit-forming if not indeed addictive, and it is doubtful that a practicing, full-fledged Witch or Warlock would fail to renew the contract so as to avoid being deprived of his powers, privileges, and skills. It is also interesting to speculate on the fate of Witches and Warlocks who do not sign a new contract. The prevalence of discoveries and Witch burnings by Men suggests that The Devil uses exposure as a retaliatory weapon against the renegade Witch or Warlock who does not want to renew the Pact. Just as gold from The Devil bursts into flame when cast on the ground, so Witches and Warlocks are set aflame when cast off by The Devil.

SABBATS

THE Sabbat is the great general assembly of Witches and Warlocks, comprised of one,

Before Streamlining

several, or hundreds of Covens. A small amount of business may be conducted at a Sabbat, but the main purpose is eating and drinking, laughing and scratching, dancing and whirling, boasting, cackling, showing off one's new red-heeled shoes and patent-leather eye patches. The Devil, or an emanation of him, attends; he is particularly fond of performing magical rites solely for the amazement and inspiration of those present.

By rule the Sabbat

begins at first stroke of midnight
is held four times yearly:
    May Eve
    All Hallows' Eve
    Candlemas
    Lammas

After Streamlining

    takes place out of doors, near water, the site having a large stone in the center and a bonfire of broken crosses over which The Devil roasts an ox
    must end at cockcrow or dawn, whichever comes first.

Box lunches may be brought. Attendance is obligatory upon all Witches and Warlocks; notice of place and time is passed from traveling Demons to Familiars, who may or may not attend.

Contrary to popular belief, it is not neces-sary to ride through the air to the Sabbat; one's mode of transport is dependent solely on the distance to be traveled and no status is lost in walking to and from if one happens to live close by. If one elects to fly, cackling and screeching on the way serve to while away the journey. The seasoned traveler will pass quietly over church steeples, however; if the bells are rung in alarm the broomstick or pitchfork will crash. It is prudent to take a small pot of extra Flying Ointment against the return journey.

ESBATS

ESBATS are the working, plenary councils of Witches and Warlocks. Because of the utilitarian nature of the Esbat they are held when need dictates and not by the calendar;

145

attendance is by invitation only and is, of course, obligatory upon receipt of the notice.

The number of those attending is held down to a workable size; Esbats of as small a number as two have been held. The Devil himself presides. Like Sabbats, Esbats commence at the first strike of midnight and cease at cockcrow or dawn.

The Esbat is concerned with conducting specific and malevolent business: harming enemies, benefiting a colleague (*i.e.*, plotting and effecting release from prison of a Witch), opening graves to obtain the bones of the unbaptized for use in making hail, or taking the fat of unbaptized infants for use in Flying Ointment. Ships are wrecked from Esbats; massive blighting of crops and cattle are effected here when the job is too great for a single Witch or Warlock.

Instruction is given by The Devil in new techniques of cursing, blasting, blighting, shriveling, withering, poxing, potioning, transforming. Familiars attend and act as assistants to The Devil during demonstrations.

Progress Reports on Private Evil-doing are mandatory; woe betide the malingerer. The Devil is a stern taskmaster and punishment for the lazy is long and painful. Treason and Backsliding are dealt with at Esbats. Execution for Treason is by hanging, beheading, or poisoning, but never by burning.

There is no fixed site for Esbats. Foul conditions are desirable: snow, rain, wind, sleet, hail, or fog always attend either singly or together. If held indoors chimneys will smoke, windows rattle, candles gutter, and timbers creak.

NOTES AND COMMENTS

WITCHES AND WARLOCKS

WARLOCKS prefer pitchforks. Witches like broomsticks.

The worst of them come from the East and the North.

They lead disorderly lives, hate salt, and cannot weep more than three tears.

Witches and Warlocks suffer
dry skin
dandruff
bunions
warts
ingrown hairs

When driven to the stake they should be made to ride in the cart seated, with a rope around their neck and wrists. Standing up in tumbrils is reserved for Aristocrats, and chains are proper only at Autos-da-Fe.

At death the body of a Witch or Warlock may

melt
dissolve
evaporate

147

A Familiar

FAMILIARS

Familiars:

Like to live in a small box of earth, a dusty pouch, or pocket.

Are fed on milk, blood, and bread. On birthdays they should be given a crumb of the Host.

Are often toads but almost never frogs.

Most often choose the form of cat or bird in preference to smaller creatures such as mice, rats, bugs, lice, which are susceptible to the careless handling of pesticides.

Are inheritable.

Wizards

TRUST those Wizards who are thin and fine drawn. Mighty muscles, ruddy cheeks, and genial dispositions bespeak Wizards who when Apprentices and young men sneaked out to play instead of applying themselves to long days over hot crucibles and long nights pouring over scrolls, tomes, tablets, and tracts.

149

Wizardry is work the like of which a Warlock has never seen. Warlocks have The Devil to help him; Wizards have only themselves. A better man than a Wizard to put your money on in a pinch can't be found. A well-trained Wizard, firm in purpose and strong in skill, will stand his ground in the face of appalling danger. Nothing is unexpected to him; his arsenal of lore was assembled on the premise that all things are likely to befall. A Wizard may have to cut and run, but he will do so judiciously, effectively, and to advantage. If you are on the same side he will very likely take you with him.

A Wizard can shape things other than they are or might be except his own doom.

He has great *savoir-faire* in the use of Spirits. He knows what to expect of them; he does not allow hesitation, backsliding, evasion, or trickery from them. Nor does he overwork them or expect them to serve him if they are occupied in the service of another, but he uses them to build or tear down edifices, reveal hidden objects, create illusions and apparitions, transport people and things. He sets Good Spirits to battle against Evil Spirits.

Wizards are not fond of working with their hands, but of necessity they manufacture magic articles if they cannot borrow or barter for them from others, or if they have no such tools handed down to them by older Wizards of yore. With the help of their Apprentices they make their own mirrors, chalk, rods, swords, and their own books of magic.

Although they may belong to Orders or Councils of other Wizards, they are not sociable or gregarious. They may be found holding appointments as Royal Wizards in the Courts of Kings, but if they remain in residence they will require a small private tower near the postern gate, and they will mingle infrequently with the Court. Their employers benefit from such divinations, prognostications, and fireworks as will leave the Wizard

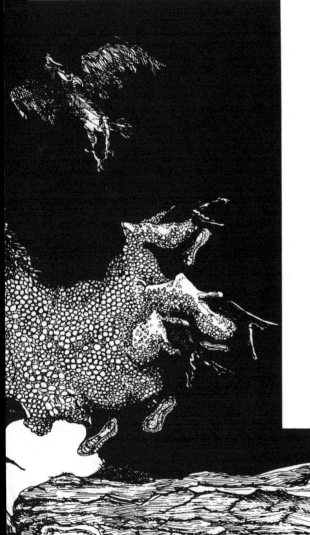

free to wander far distances on his own pursuits much of the time.

They have excellent vision, particularly when their eyes are closed, and prefer above all things living in high places with unobstructed views, many bookshelves, and room to pace.

Wizards have favorite colors; they tend to gray eyes and are either clean-shaven or fully bearded. They are impatient and nervous, cool-headed in face of danger, and choleric when presented with incompetence or stupidity. They may take new names from time to time.

When traveling, Wizards at least half the time are disguised, usually wearing a cloak of sober hue, a soft, wide-brimmed hat, and an eye patch, carrying a staff, and stooping. They are touchingly fond of casting off this impenetrable disguise and revealing themselves at opportune moments. Transformations are child's play to them but do not seem to satisfy their love of dressing up as disguises do.

Wizards are not immortal, but they are extremely durable and last many centuries.

The very skills and arts which a Wizard perfects and uses for the benefit of others and for his own benevolent projects are fell weapons to match when turned to evil ends. After centuries of straightening out, adjusting, rescuing, and setting to rights the affairs of the world, a Wizard may begin to think he is better equipped to run the world than anyone

else. If he succumbs to this urge he is a formidable opponent to put down. A good Wizard is forced to hold himself and his magic in check a bit—ride a little less swiftly, blast a little less blisteringly, smite less shatteringly than he is able in order not to slay idle bystanders. But when the welfare of others is no longer his concern, the full force of his power may be felt and much woe unleashed into the world.

But the very elements which he so perfectly controlled for good will in time turn against him. He will eventually no longer be able to call on the free services of Dwarves, Spirits, Elves, and other former allies, for the guise of innocence assumed by a corrupt Wizard is transparent to them.

A corrupt Wizard, his influence diminishing, may make a Pact with The Devil in order to regain his former powers by use of Evil Spirits. In this case he becomes an Arch-Warlock and ceases to be a Wizard altogether.

GENERAL TRENDS

Wizards

appear when least expected

are always in a hurry

don't stay long

speak all tongues, including those of birds and beasts

fear few things and are equal to most of them

can foretell and divine without the use of apparatus either by closing their eyes or by looking at the horizon

can be tricked

can trick you

prefer standing to sitting, and pacing to standing

can with perfect etiquette demand a service from you in return for the one you ask of them, and you must perform yours first

must perform their own rites

are always a little overworked

USEFUL INFORMATION

including

Legal Holidays

Weights and Measures

Simples, Specifics, and Sovereign Remedies

LEGAL HOLIDAYS

January	1		*Horses' birthdays*
	6		*Twelfth Night*
	20		*Eve of Ste. Agnes*
February	2	s	*Candlemas*
March	25	Q	*Lady Day*
April	30	s	*Walpurgis Night*
May	1	s	*Beltane*
	1		*May Day*
	3	s	*Roodmas*
June	23	s	*Midsummer Eve*
	23		*St. John's Eve*
	24	Q	*Midsummer Day*
July	15		*St. Swithin's Day*
	31	s	*Lammas Eve*
August	1	s	*Lammas*
September	8		*Lady Day*
	29	Q	*Michaelmas*
October	31	s	*All Hallow's Eve*
November	1		*All Saints' Day*
	2		*All Souls' Day*
December	21		*St. Thomas' Day*
December	25	sQ	*Yule*
December	28		*Lady Day*

s: Sabbats likely
Q: Quarter Day

Whitsuntide: 7 weeks following Easter
Whitsunday: 7 weeks and one day following Easter
Shrove Tuesday: the Tuesday before Ash Wednesday
Maundy Thursday: the Thursday before Good Friday

REPUBLICAN CALENDAR

1 *Vendémiaire*	22 September	VINTAGE
1 *Brumaire*	22 October	FOG
1 *Frimaire*	21 November	FROST
1 *Nivôse*	21 December	SNOW
1 *Pluviôse*	20 January	RAIN
1 *Ventôse*	19 February	WIND
1 *Germinal*	21 March	BUDS
1 *Floréal*	20 April	FLOWERS
1 *Prairial*	20 May	MEADOWS
1 *Messidor*	19 June	REAPING
1 *Thermidor*	19 July	HEAT
1 *Fructidor*	18 August	FRUIT

ROMAN NUMERALS

I	1	L	50
II	2	LX	60
III	3	LXX	70
IIII or IV	4	LXXX	80
V	5	XC	90
VI	6	C	100
VII	7	D	500
VIII	8	M	1,000
IX	9	$\bar{V}$	5,000
X	10	$\bar{X}$	10,000
XX	20	$\bar{L}$	50,000
XXII	22	$\bar{C}$	100,000
XXX	30	$\bar{D}$	500,000
XL	40	$\bar{M}$	1,000,000

WEIGHTS

Stone	14 pounds
Firkin	56 pounds
Clove	7-10 pounds
Kip	half a ton
Pennyweight	24 grains
Hundredweight	112 pounds
Fardel	4 Cloves
Burthen	1 Firkin plus 1 Stone

MEASURES

Palm	3 inches
Hand	4 inches
Span	9 inches
Cubit	18 inches
Pace	2½ feet
Ell	4 feet
Fathom	5½ yards
Pole, Rod (Perch)	6 feet
Furlong	220 yards
Cable	120 fathoms
League	3 miles
Se'nnight	1 week
Fortnight	2 weeks
Widdershins	countersunwise

Noggin or Gill:	¼ pint
Firkin	½ kilderkin
Runlet	a scant kilderkin
Kilderkin	2 firkins, ¼ tun
Barrel	31.5 gallons (U.S.)
Hogshead	2 barrels
Pipe or Butt	2 hogshead, ½ tun, 4 barrels
Puncheon	if wine, 84 gallons
	if beer or ale, 72 gallons
Tun	2 pipes, 4 hogsheads, 8 barrels if wine, 252 gallons

COSTREL

EWER

PIGGIN
PIPKIN

FLAGON

FLASKS

BEAKER

GOBLET

MORTAR

TANKARD

157

UMMER

TUMBLER

HORN

BLACKJACK

STEIN

MAZERS

VIALS & PHIALS

VESSLES & PESTLE

CANONICAL HOURS

Matins and Lauds: between midnight and dawn
Prime: 6 AM
Tierce: 9 AM
Sext: 12 noon
None: 3 PM
Vespers: before nightfall
Compline: before bed

SACRAMENTS

Baptism
Confirmation
Ordination
Marriage
Penance
Eucharist
Extreme Unction

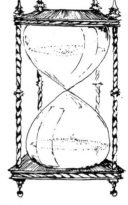

DEADLY SINS

Avarice, Gluttony, Sloth, Pride, Envy, Lust, Anger

SPLENDID VIRTUES

Faith, Hope, Charity, Justice, Prudence, Fortitude, Temperance

PERTINENT SEAS

Mediterranean, Red, Chinese, West African, East African, Indian, Persian

PLEIADES

Alcyone, Celaeno, Electra, Merope, Sterope, Taygeta, Maia

SEVEN WONDERS

Tomb of Mausolus
Lighthouse at Alexandria
Temple of Diana at Ephesus
Pyramids
Hanging Gardens of Babylon
Statue of Zeus at Olympia
Colossus of Rhodes

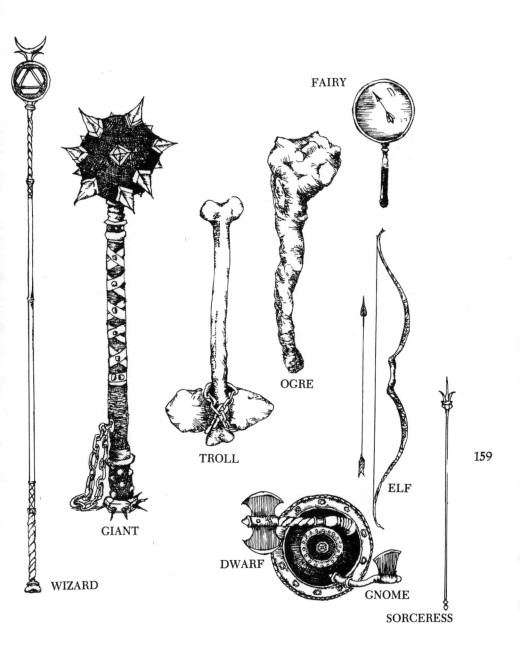

FAIRY

GIANT

TROLL

OGRE

WIZARD

DWARF

GNOME

ELF

SORCERESS

159

SIMPLES, SPECIFICS, AND SOVEREIGN REMEDIES

EPILEPSY: Dissolve one pearl in one wineglass (4 tablespoons) of vinegar or lemon juice and drink.
Bathe Epileptics as often as possible in human blood.

WARTS: Rub Warts with green elder stick and bury stick in mud. Warts will disappear.
Rub Warts daily with vinegar.
Bathe Warts in rainwater found in hollow tree stump.

FEVER: Seal live bedbug in hollow bean and swallow. Liquor from toads boiled in oil also helps reduce Fever.

DEAFNESS, NIGHT BLINDNESS: Boil or fry right eye of hedgehog and steep it in oil in a brazen vessel for several months. Apply resulting salve to affected organ.

HEADACHES: Take tea made from tansy or vervain.

LEPROSY: Bathe Lepers daily in human blood.

RHEUMATISM: Boil one frog in vinegar, reduce liquid, and use for liniment.
Dandelion tea is said to be helpful.

CONSUMPTION: Swallow whole one tongue taken from live lizard.

MOUTH RASHES: Burn to ash in oven leaves of holly, mix with honey, and take as syrup until condition disappears.

COLDS AND RHEUMS: Take tea made from root, not bark, of sassafras tree.

INFECTED OPEN WOUNDS: Poultices of cobwebs and soot must be applied promptly and kept fresh until danger has passed. Moulded bread may be substituted in the absence of cobwebs.

MUSCULAR ACHES AND PAINS: For relief of Pain where skin is not broken, make a linseed poultice of 4 parts crushed linseed, 1 part mustard, soaked in boiling water. Spread between two flannels and place hot on site of Pain. Bran or hops may replace linseed, and turpentine may be substituted for mustard.

SCORPION BITES: Prevent Scorpion Bites by wearing forget-me-nots.

SPLINTERS: To extract deep-seated Splinters, place highly salted meat or bacon over opening and keep moist and warm until head of Splinter appears and can be extracted.
(See also *Bleeding,
Gore* and *Hazards of the Course*)